Howard Carter:

From Tracer to Tutankhamun

Howard Carter:

From Tracer to Tutankhamun

Spotlight on EES.ART.224

by

Carl Graves

Series editor:
Stephanie Boonstra

Foreword

> *... remember that I am an artist & cannot see what way digging for antiquities should advance me in my future career.*
>
> Howard Carter to Francis Llewelyn Griffith, 1893

Howard Carter is synonymous with Tutankhamun, their fates so intertwined that we sometimes find it difficult to separate the 'discoverer' from the discovery. Overshadowed by his later success, we often forget about Carter's back catalogue of work as an Egyptologist, archaeologist, and artist-cum-illustrator. In fact, it is Carter's tome of artwork that I am most taken with, his talent and skill as an artist that gave him a break into the privileged world of archaeology at the end of the 19th century.

If you've ever had the pleasure to see his artistry, the assured sleek lines and vivid hues spread across thick white linen paper to form into images of birds, gods, and proud queens, confidently depicting ancient Egyptian scenes and intricate snapshots of paintings from forgotten tombs. Delicately inked watercolours race across the page, transporting the admirer to past landscapes and the ancient people who created them. Within each piece you can feel Carter's concentration, his keen-eye honed onto singular detail, recording remnants of the past with precision.

Carter's first employment in Egypt was under the auspices of the Egypt Exploration Society; he was just seventeen years old and even then he showed tenacity to better the field of archaeology, which was still in its infancy. How to record, illustrate, and retain information was largely unknown and very much a labour of trial by error. Carter was one of the first to create schematic drawings of how archaeological sites were uncovered and preserved, adamant to show the reality of erosion and damage in his drawings. Perfection in the imperfection – no doubt influenced by his artistic training in his formative years by his father, a great artist himself.

Fundamentally, Carter's system and methodology are the foundations of archaeological technique today. Archaeologists from around the world employ the same methods to ensure preservation by record. I have no doubt that Carter's eye for 'wonderful things' led to his meticulous mindset, enabling him to transfer these skills to create a systematic process for excavation, recording and conservation.

Howard Carter's final masterpiece is undoubtedly his archives, including those of KV62 – Tutankhamun's tomb. His records are sleek and sublime, enabling the reader to retrace the excavations. Breath-taking illustrations and photographic records come into their own, showing us that he was an early adopter of technology with the ability to transfer his knowledge and eye for rigorous detail to his wider excavation team.

Every year our knowledge of science and technology widens, enabling the modern field of archaeology to answer deeper questions of our past. Within that we often forget that that Archaeology is a dual discipline comprising of art and science. This volume captures the spirit of that notion, wrapped and embodied in Howard Carter's earlier artwork, a timely reminder that one cannot independently thrive without the other.

Raksha Dave, May 2024

Timeline

Major milestones in the career of Howard Carter.

May 1874
- Born in Brompton, Kensington before relocating to Sporle Road, Swaffham in Norfolk.

October 1891
- Appointed by the Egypt Exploration Fund (EEF) as 'tracer' for the Archaeological Survey of Egypt working at Beni Hasan and Deir el-Bersha.

1892
- Trained by William Matthew Flinders Petrie at Amarna.

1893
- Recording at Sheikh Said and Mendes (Timai el-Amdid). Then appointed as deputy to Édouard Naville at Deir el-Bahari for the EEF.

1899
- Resigned from his work for the EEF to take up the role of Chief Inspector of Upper Egyptian Antiquities for the Service des Antiquités de l'Égypte by Gaston Maspero alongside James Edward Quibell for Lower Egypt.
- Took up residence in 'Castle Carter' near Medinet Habu.

1900
- Excavated Bab el-Hosan (Gate of the Horse) in front of the Mentuhotep Nebhepetre mortuary temple at Deir el-Bahari.
- Cleared KV42 with Chinouda Macarios and Boutros Andraos.

1901
- The robbery of KV35, the tomb of Amenhotep II.

1903
- Discovery of the tomb of Tuthmosis IV (KV43) financed by Theodore Davis.

1904
- Relocated to the inspectorate of Lower Egypt in Cairo.

1905
- The 'Saqqara Affair'. Relocated to Tanta. In October, Carter resigned from the Service des Antiquités and moved back to Luxor.

1909
- Began working with Lord Carnarvon at Sheikh Abd el-Qurna and Dra Abu el-Naga.

1914
- Davis leaves the concession at the Valley of the Kings and it is passed on to Lord Carnarvon. Carter begins a systematic clearance of the wadi floor to record worker's huts and find any missing tombs.

1915
- Carter catalogued the collection of the Amherst family, ready for sale in Sotheby's.

1916
- Began the epigraphic recording of the Opet Festival scenes at the Luxor Temple for Alan Gardiner.

4th November 1922
- The first step of an undiscovered tomb was found. Tomb of Tutankhamun discovered.

25th November 1922
- Sealed entrance of the tomb removed and the first glimpse of 'wonderful things'.

1923
- Lord Carnarvon dies and the concession is passed onto Lady Carnarvon (Almina Herbert).

1925
- Opening of Tutankhamun's coffins and revelation of the golden mask.

1929
- Carter negotiates compensation for the Carnarvon family from the Egyptian Government.

1932
- Clearance of the tomb of Tutankhamun was finally completed.

1939
- Howard Carter died of cancer in London at his flat at 49 Albert Road, Kensington.

Maps

Map of Egypt

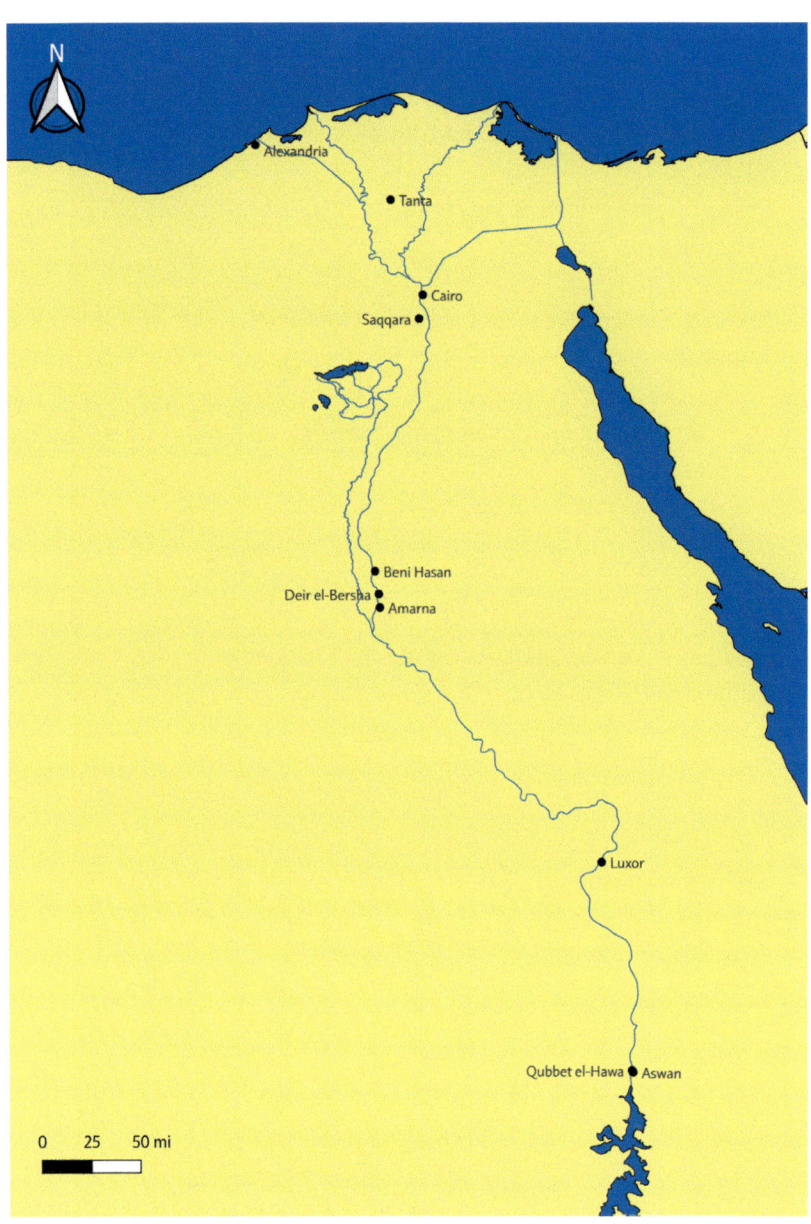

Theban West Bank

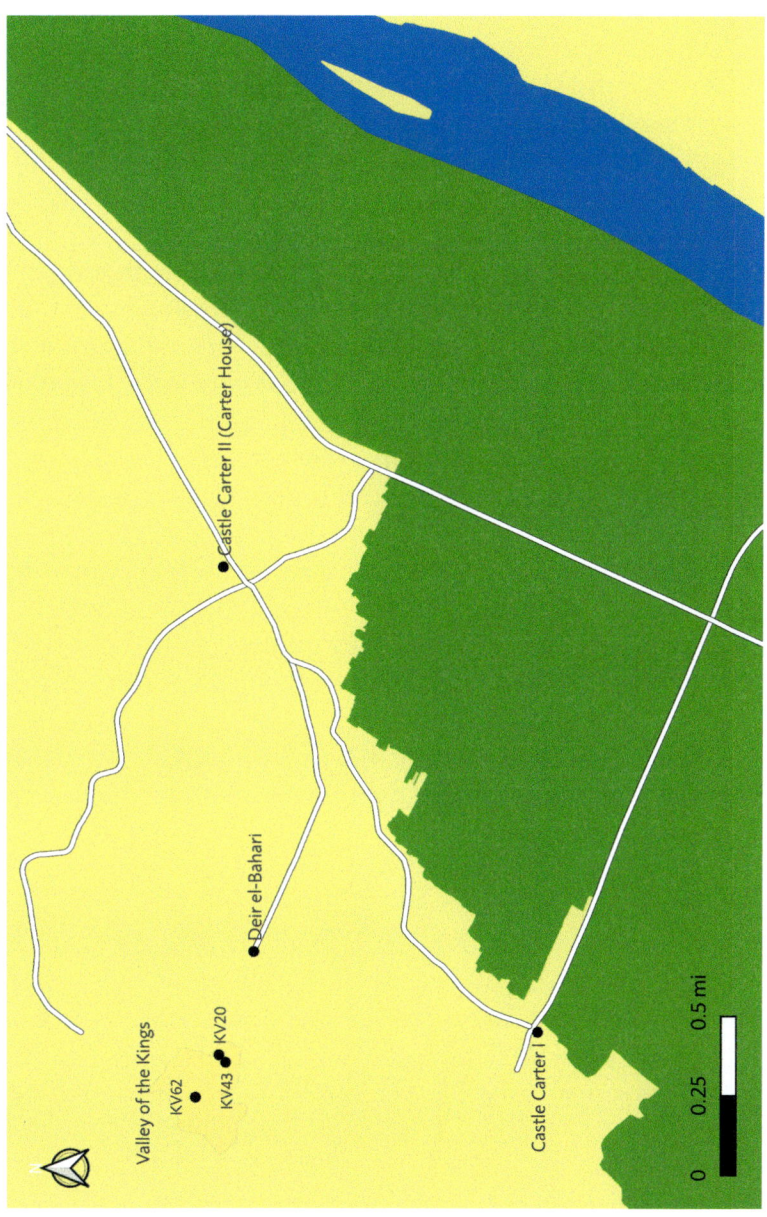

Acknowledgements

Even a short book like this takes time to put together but is never the work of one person alone. I'd like to thank my friends in the EES archives for inspiring me to explore them further and also being so generous with their time and knowledge. In particular, I am grateful to Brigitte Balanda and John Wyatt for their friendship over the years together in the archives investigating, among many other things, Howard Carter's early career at the EES. I'd like to offer my sincere gratitude to Andrew and Emma Sutcliffe, Tony Marks, Rupert Wace, William Joy (Peggy Joy Egyptology Library), Paul Nicholson, and Angela Reid for sharing their collections with me and, where requested, allowing me to reproduce images. My colleagues and friends at the Griffith Institute deserve so much appreciation for their patience with the (many) enquiries sent their way and their very generous permission to use images from their collections; I only hope to one day repay the favour. It is thanks to a generous donation from Winsor & Newton, original suppliers of the watercolour paints used by the Archaeological Survey of Egypt in 1890, that the first print-run of this volume was completed, enriching our understanding of their own contribution to the history of Egyptology. I am also thankful to the generous support of The Vanellus Trust for making the production of this volume possible.

To Jack, I'd like to express my thanks – for finally proofreading something I wrote! And, to my dear friend Sarah for doing a final professional read over everything. Of course, to the reviewers for their kind words and suggestions which have improved the work. Any mistakes left remain my own.

Finally, and it should always go without saying, it is with thanks to members of the Egypt Exploration Society (past, present, and future!) that the production of these volumes and all the work that we do is possible. Thank you all.

Carl Graves, April 2024.

Introduction

This spotlight volume is intended to provide historical context to one of the most impressive items in the collections of the Egypt Exploration Society by exploring the life of its painter, Howard Carter – one of the most famous and yet often misunderstood characters of British Egyptology.

The painting long stood in the London Office of the Society providing a backdrop to general operations as well as various retirement or leaving parties. It has been a first-hand witness to the activities of the EES since its creation in 1894, welcoming visitors and saying farewell to those that have played important roles in the history of Egyptology. But its presence has often been taken for granted and its own role in our history somewhat forgotten. This volume corrects this oversight and sheds new light on this masterpiece of archaeological recording. It is not intended as a biography of Carter and the author directs readers to the accomplished example by T G H James (1992). Nor is it an account of the discovery of the tomb of Tutankhamun, in fact you will find very little here and much written in other volumes (see further reading). This volume, instead, focuses on Carter's earlier career, largely under the employ of the Egypt Exploration Fund (now Society) and those skills that, ultimately, led to the greatest archaeological discovery in the Valley of the Kings.

The main focus is, of course, the watercolour – EES.ART.224. Interest in the painting was reignited in 2022 when celebrations for the centenary of the discovery of Tutankhamun's tomb were being planned. Taking a slightly different approach, the Visions of Ancient Egypt exhibition at the Sainsbury Centre in Norwich displayed the painting to show the ways in which artwork, like that of Carter, had inspired modern views on ancient Egypt. Before loaning the painting, it first required conservation. The Society was particularly fortunate to receive a generous donation for this to be carried out prior to that loan. In carrying out this much-needed care, more information about the painting came to light which subsequently led to greater research in Carter's history at the EES.

This research, in turn, led to a special EES Member's Tour in October 2022, 'In the footsteps of Howard Carter'. Together with the author, 22 Members explored some of the sites that became influential in Carter's development as an archaeologist such as Beni Hasan, Deir el-Bersha, Amarna, and, of course, Luxor and the Valley of the Kings. Today, in 2024, EES.ART.224 is on loan to institutions around the UK where it will be complemented by artefacts in their own collections before it returns to Doughty Mews for display alongside the Society's other collections. The EES is grateful to all those who have worked on this project at various institutions and who continue to support its work in Egypt by becoming members and making donations.

The Early Years, 1874–1890

Howard Carter was born on 9th May 1874 at 10 Rich Terrace, Brompton, Kensington. In later autobiographical sketches, however, he would tell people that he was born in Swaffham, Norfolk. This may have been intended to give himself an air of the country and the impression of a slightly better upbringing. At the time, Kensington was not particularly affluent and was yet to undergo the vast transformation during the Victorian period that can be seen today. Carter would, in his later years, return to this area and died in his apartment there in 1939.

It was in Swaffham that Samuel John Carter and Martha Joyce (nee Sands) raised their ten sons and one daughter. Though living in a small rural cottage on a larger estate, they made regular trips back to London and retained a property there. Not much is known of Martha Joyce Carter, but Howard would later recollect 'A small, kindly woman [who] loved luxury. A weakness also inherited by her youngest son.'[1] Howard's letters to his mother (or 'Mater' as he often addressed her) demonstrate their close relationship and he regularly kept her informed of his activities.

Samuel John Carter, Howard's father, was a prolific artist who specialised in painting fauna (both domestic and wild) as well as sporting scenes such as hunting. He won several awards for his work at the Royal Academy and regularly exhibited there between 1855 and 1890. The Carter family background in painting was instilled in some of his children, including Howard and his brothers, Vernet (also spelled Verney) and William. A large oil painting of Howard Carter, today in the Griffith Institute, University of Oxford, was painted by William Carter and shows Howard in his later years after his most famous discovery.

Carter's training as an artist began at an early age. Already, in the 1891 census, Howard is listed as living in Kensington, with his parents, three siblings, and one domestic servant. He is described as an 'art student'. Though Carter's biographers have noted that his formal schooling is unclear, he must have received some professional guidance either in a school or via his father and brothers. At the time of the 1891 census, Howard was 16 years old and would shortly travel to Egypt.

Howard's journey to Egypt was driven through his relationship with a local wealthy family – the Tyssen-Amhersts, clients of Howard's father. William Tyssen-Amherst (more properly, Baron William Amhurst Tyssen-Amherst, 1st Baron Amherst of Hackney, 1835–1909) was a keen collector of antiquities and had established a small private museum at his home in Norfolk called Didlington Hall. His wife, Margaret Susan Amherst (nee Mitford,

1 Swaffham today. The original 'Pedlar of Swaffham' road sign that greets visitors to the town was actually painted by Henry Robert (Harry) Carter, a distant cousin of Howard himself. Image by author.

2 Presented to the Right Honourable Jacob Henry Delaval Lord Hastings by 400 of his Friends and Neighbours at Melton Constable [Hall] on the 7th of November 1865, *attributed to Samuel John Carter. Courtesy of Andrew and Emma Sutcliffe.*

3 Snailspit Farm, Cley Road, Swaffham, Norfolk, *Samuel John Carter*. STC1. Copyright Swaffham Town Hall.

4 *Oil painting of Howard Carter by his brother William Carter, 1924. Carter MSS viii.2. Copyright Griffith Institute, University of Oxford.*

5   *Didlington Hall, home of the Tyssen-Amhersts. The seven Sekhmet statues can be seen to the right of the image looking over the gardens. Copyright Angela Reid.*

1835–1919) was a prolific correspondent and was heavily involved in the affairs of her husband's collecting.

The estate of the Amherst's naturally attracted scholars, including Egyptologists. One, Percy Newberry (1868–1949), started visiting in his late teens during the 1880s. Newberry is remembered as an archaeologist, but he also studied botany and was visiting Didlington Hall to provide advice on botanical specimens. His experience and archaeological training meant that, in 1890, the Egypt Exploration Fund (EEF, now Egypt Exploration Society, EES) appointed him to lead their epigraphical mission to Beni Hasan as part of the recently launched Archaeological Survey of Egypt.

The EEF had been founded in 1882 by the Victorian novelist and travel writer, Amelia B Edwards. Its mission was to excavate and preserve (through the keeping of scientific records) the archaeological sites of Egypt. It continues today, as the EES, to support and promote Egyptian cultural heritage. The

> *Epigraphy:*
> Carved and/or painted decoration often found on the temple and tomb walls of ancient Egypt as well as mobile artworks such as stelae and statuary. An epigrapher would record these scenes to interpret their meaning, context, and development over time. In Egypt, epigraphy can include both writing (hieroglyphs, hieratic, etc.) as well as art which are often difficult to disentangle. While Carter was considered a 'tracer' or artist working for the EEF, today his role would be as an epigrapher, accurately recording the reliefs and decoration found on the monuments.

Archaeological Survey of Egypt was the idea of Francis Llewellyn Griffith (1862–1934) who first suggested 'a rapid sketch-survey' of the whole country at an Annual General Meeting of the Egypt Exploration Fund in 1889:[2]

> With the countenance and support of the Egyptian Government, we might in a few years sweep the whole surface of the country, and gather in the harvest which hastens to ruin with every day that passes. But what would be most useful and most practicable? Egypt has already been industriously searched by travellers and scientific expeditions. The efforts of the French School at Cairo and of independent tourists are not relaxing. What is needed is a sifting of information, an index to the monuments, a description from a new point of view, taking each city, its tombs and temples, as a whole, and not merely extracting scenes, inscriptions, and architectural features. The latter method was wisely enough followed in former days, when our knowledge of the country, its history and habits, was almost *nil*, when the harvest was abundant to overflowing, but the workmen few, and the most striking and choice pieces alone could be gathered.

An unpretentious, but very effective, way of making a survey would be, simply to secure the services of one or two persons who should, as a preliminary, make themselves acquainted with the whole literature of Egyptian exploration, should possess a knowledge of Arabic, and be capable of taking photographs. The programme would be, for the explorers to pass from end to end of the country, from Migdol to Syene, from Iskenderiyeh to El Arish, verifying the accounts of travellers, collecting place-names, searching out new monuments, and describing the order and condition of those already known; and, after issuing temporary reports and monographs, finally gathering all the evidence into one connected survey, to which everyone could confidently refer who might wish to learn the position and condition of any monument, what was known about it, in what works other and more

6 *Percy Newberry at the site of Beni Hasan with three unnamed Egyptian team members. Courtesy of the Egypt Exploration Society.*

detailed accounts might be found, and how far investigation was still needed. The friendly criticism of scholars all over the world might be invited; and the stores of information which lie hidden in MS. [manuscript] collections in various parts of Europe would thus be brought together for the production of a work which, as a stimulus and guide, would be invaluable. It would be one of the foundations of all further research, would prevent much of that misapplication of labour which is almost unavoidable for the best-read explorer, and would point out to the casual traveller aims to which his energies might be applied with the most useful results.

The cost of the scheme might be estimated at from £100 to £250 a year for each person employed; an explorer living constantly in Egypt would not find his mere expenses rise much above the former sum. I am not sure that this scheme would interfere with the annual excavations. Even if it did so, on its completion the Members of the Society would resume their first method of discovery, with the satisfactory assurance that they had done their best for those relics of the past which unhappily never received the kindly protection that nature has extended to so many, by hiding them under sand, rubbish, and alluvium.

I believe that two years would be ample for a thoroughly useful sketch-survey; i.e. for the verification, numbering, and cataloguing of the remains, with slight but accurate descriptions, and for bringing together the literary references. What a mass of misapprehension would disappear! What a crowd of new revelations would dawn upon the science of Egyptology from this alone! But I hardly believe that the Exploration Fund would relinquish this vastly-interesting field until it had with its own hand, so to speak, filled in many of the details that were hardly indicated by the sketch.

Both Reginald Stuart Poole (Honorary Secretary of the Fund) and Sir John Fowler (President of the Fund) both heartily endorsed Griffith's proposal, largely owing to his moderate estimate of costs and its ambitious coverage. At the next year's annual General Meeting, Griffith reported on the progress of the Survey which had, by then, employed Percy Newberry as Director of the work in Egypt and amended its, initially, over-ambitious plans. A specific region in Middle Egypt focusing on the east bank sites around Beni Hasan had been selected rather than the entirety of the Nile valley. Newberry was assisted by George Willoughby Fraser (1866–1923, an engineer with an archaeological background) and Marcus Worseley Blackden (1864–1934, an artist) copying, tracing, and photographing the scenes and inscriptions at Beni Hasan in Middle Egypt:[3]

> It is with feelings of unmixed gratitude to the great Society which has accepted and fostered a timidly-suggested scheme, that I have the honour to present the first Report of the Archaeological Survey of Egypt. […]
>
> It is not difficult for one who has studied Egyptian archaeology in the country for some years to see what is required in order that the archaeological inheritance of so many centuries may not be swept away at the very moment when the world appears ready to receive and appreciate it. What can be done to stem the torrent of absolute destruction? Here and there a single tomb or temple can be put under lock and key by the action of the Government, or some learned society may undertake- its restoration. But history, science and art demand more than this. The Nile valley contains a multitude of monuments and ruins, – some partly described, some as yet almost unknown, but all alike exposed to the attacks of the dealer in antiquities, the quarryman and the wanton iconoclast. To collect all the information, that can be gathered from all extant monuments appears to be the first step to take in this direction. Underground lie other stores of knowledge in the buried monuments, safe from all but the excavator's spade, and reserved for the enterprise of posterity. Lastly come the small antiquities, which when comprehended are not less instructive, and are much more unfailing than the

monuments. These have only now begun to speak to the world, and their silent evidence is swept away wholesale from day to day.

But a systematic archaeological survey of the monuments is now commenced, and will furnish the best answer to the question propounded above. If the originals must vanish, they can at least be classified; and plans and copies can, with time, money, and perseverance, be made of all. These copies can be rendered available for students in a space of moderate dimensions, while their publication on a reduced scale will hasten the rapid progress of Egyptological science and research.

In November, 1889, the General Meeting approved the suggestion of an Archaeological Survey of Egypt. The idea present in my mind at that time was a rapid sketch-survey, to result in an elaborate catalogue of monuments, with references to all publications, the object being to point out in detail what work had been accomplished and what still required to be done.

For many months the matter remained at a standstill. No one appeared ready to undertake the work. At length Mr. Fraser, who had not only manifested great interest in Egyptian antiquities, but had sent me copies of some important inscriptions from the neighbourhood of Minyeh, was engaged by the Egypt Exploration Fund to prepare a large block for removal from Tell Basta. His offer to assist in the excavations, or in the survey, followed, and was accepted.

At this juncture Mr. Newberry also volunteered to take up the work.

We first planned a sketch-survey from Minyeh to Siut (Assyut). Our endeavour to prepare for this survey showed the impossibility of attaining any satisfactory result. Mr. Newberry then proposed to take up a small district and treat it exhaustively, which seemed to me the only practicable and satisfactory course. We then selected a district which contained three well-known groups of monuments, namely: certain tombs of the VIth Dynasty at Kum-el-Ahmar, opposite Minyeh on the north; the celebrated group of Beni Hasan tombs to the southward (XIIth

Dynasty); and, two miles farther up the river, the grottoes of Speos Artemidos (XVIIIth Dynasty). The district is only fifteen miles long. The above monuments are excavated in the eastern cliffs, but the western bank has scarcely been explored at all.

For this little section of the valley of the Nile, we thoroughly examined at the British Museum all works of authority, both published and in manuscript. It is, however, doubtful whether the whole of the present season will not be occupied in copying one single group of monuments. At Beni Hasan are thirty-nine tombs, twelve of which are inscribed, while eight of these twelve are not only inscribed but painted. The rest are plain, but there are altogether twelve thousand square feet of painted wall-surface. The outlines of these paintings are blurred, the colours are dim, and all the surfaces are defaced by the bats, the smoke, the graffiti of modern tourists, the wanton injuries inflicted by the natives, and the oils and other preparations of former copyists.

All these twelve thousand square feet have to be puzzled out and the colours identified, while a faithful transcript, of which every detail is of as much importance as the *ensemble*, must be made by means of tracing-paper.

Let him who would realise what this means mount a ladder and trace a fresco in one of our ancient churches. He will then appreciate the steady devotion of the copyist to his task of twelve thousand square feet.

The paintings are in a worse state than they were fifty years ago, [...].

Mr. Newberry started from England on November 5th [1890], taking with him annotated tracings, photographs, and copies of all the published scenes and inscriptions necessary for his purpose. On the 25th he reached Beni Hasan, and, thanks to Mr. Fraser's knowledge of the country and the people, had no difficulty in settling down for his first campaign. The tombs in Egypt have often afforded pleasant and secure lodging for explorers. In this case an uninscribed tomb, " No. 15," [sic] has been " adapted."

> Selected portions of the Beni Hasan inscriptions were long ago copied with great accuracy by Lepsius. Hay's copies are also good, and suggested to me some important emendations, some of which are now verified. The progress of science and the rectification of the copies will enable us to give a much improved account of them. It is intended to copy carefully a specimen of every coloured hieroglyph; and in the scenes, the colours of all important details will be reproduced. By this means much light will be thrown on the origin of hieroglyphic signs, and on the nature of the objects depicted. Mr. Blackden, an artist who has turned his attention to Egyptian subjects with great success, is now assisting Mr. Newberry in the colouring.

Sent out with Blackden was a request for 'a series of Winsor and Newton's water colour paints' and '3 quires of Whatman's hotpressed drawing paper'. These simple, but high-quality supplies would become the principal tools of the Archaeological Survey's work.

The rock-cut tomb chapels of Beni Hasan date from the First Intermediate Period and early Middle Kingdom (c. 2160–1831 BCE). Alongside the 39 chapels in the upper necropolis (12 of which are decorated), more than 800 shaft tombs cover the lower necropolis escarpment. The tomb chapels belonged to the governors (or Nomarchs) of the local region (or Nome), local elites, and high officials. Griffith estimated that

7 *Francis Llewellyn Griffith, the founder of the Archæological Survey of Egypt. Courtesy of the Egypt Exploration Society.*

there were 1,115 m² of decorated scenes to record. These scenes included brightly coloured representations of daily life along the Nile valley during the Pharaonic Period and remain some of the most dynamic and lively preserved from the early Middle Kingdom. The inscriptions provide biographical information about the administration of an ancient Egyptian province and the activities of the elite in that region. The Survey team were tasked with faithfully recording these scenes and inscriptions ready for publication. Following the first season of work in 1890–91, it was clear that further assistance would be required to complete the task.

On his return to the UK, Newberry must have mentioned the need for further artists to Lady Amherst during one of his visits to Didlington Hall. She then wrote to Amelia Edwards at the EEF suggesting that the young Howard Carter might be a suitable appointment. The Amhersts even offered to cover his salary to the value of £100.

On 16th October 1891, it was resolved by the Fund's Committee that 'Mr Carter be appointed as Tracer to assist Mr Newberry at a cost not exceeding £50'. It might be assumed that the remaining

8 *The terrace of tomb chapels in the Upper Necropolis of Beni Hasan. Image by author.*

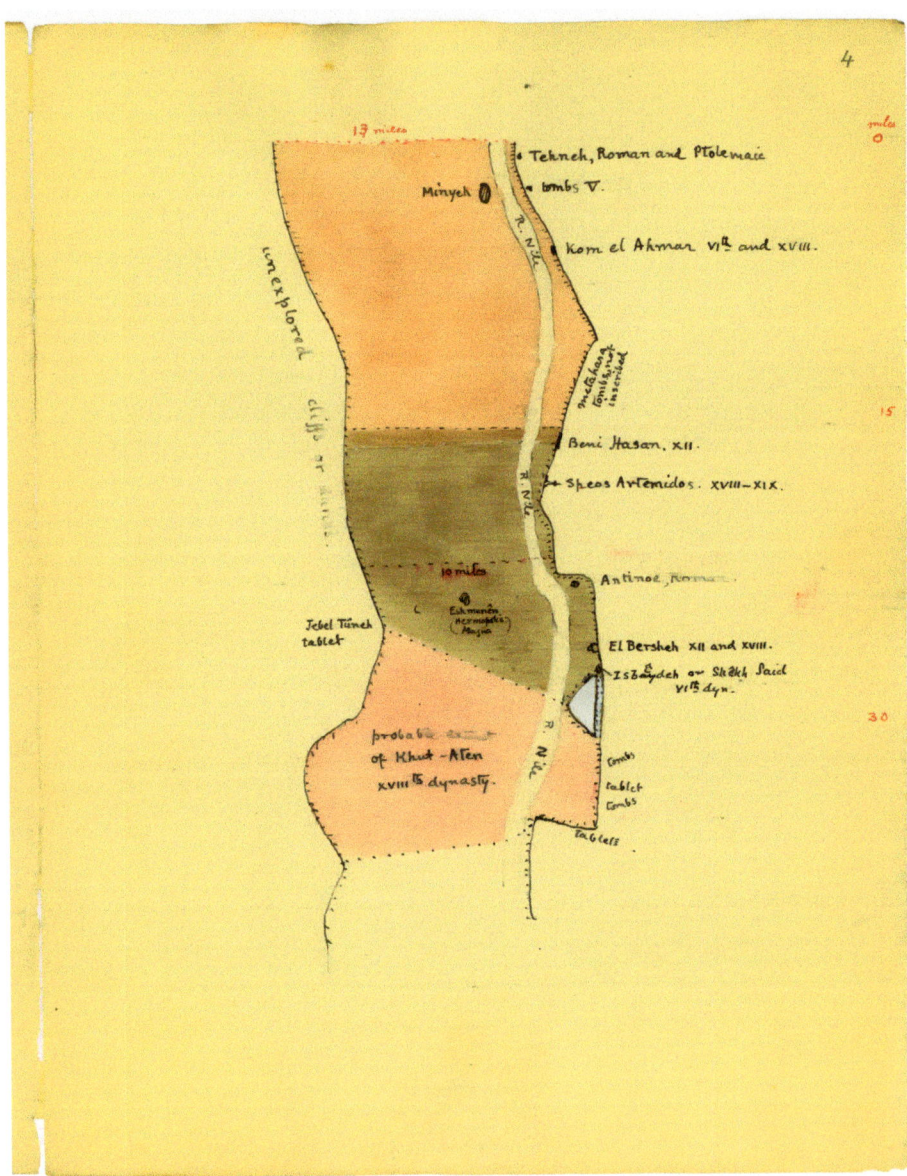

9 A map of Middle Egypt showing the area to be covered by the EEF Archaeological Survey of Egypt between el-Minya in the north and Mallawi in the south. EES.COR.06.j.01. Courtesy of the Egypt Exploration Society.

funds offered by the Amhersts were used to cover Carter's travel and accommodation expenses. Over the course of his work, Newberry would also be assisted by his brother, John, and Percy Buckman alongside Fraser, Blackman, and Carter.

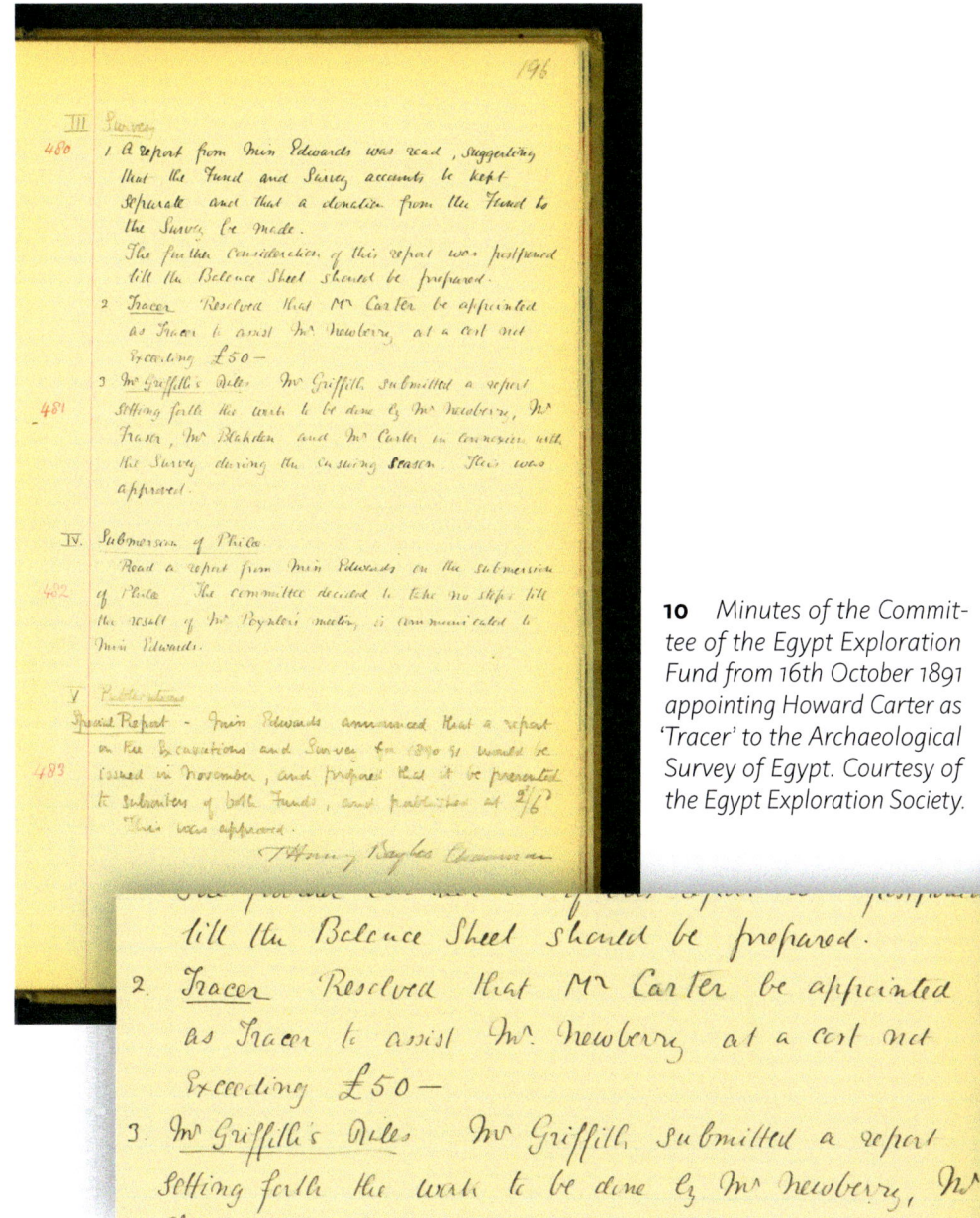

10 Minutes of the Committee of the Egypt Exploration Fund from 16th October 1891 appointing Howard Carter as 'Tracer' to the Archaeological Survey of Egypt. Courtesy of the Egypt Exploration Society.

From artist to archaeologist, 1891–1899

Shortly after the Committee's decision, Carter travelled alone to Egypt from London after his father dropped him off at Victoria Station. He was just 17 when he arrived, by boat, sometime in late October or early November 1891. Newberry met him in Alexandria and they travelled to Cairo together. Here, Carter visited the Museum of Egyptian Antiquities which had recently opened in a Khedival Palace at Giza following the flooding and closure of the original Boulaq Museum established by Auguste Mariette in 1858. He also spent several evenings conversing with William Matthew Flinders Petrie (1853–1942), the foremost British archaeologist working in Egypt at the time. He would later reflect that these meetings were formative for him, though he was not to know at the time how dramatically his life would change over the coming year.

On arriving at Beni Hasan, Newberry, Fraser, Blackden, and

11 *The interior of tomb-chapel 16 at Beni Hasan once converted into living accommodation for Percy Newberry in 1892. Courtesy of the Egypt Exploration Society.*

12 *The exterior of tomb-chapel 16 at Beni Hasan. Image by author.*

Carter set up camp in tomb number 16 in the upper necropolis.[4] The tomb was undecorated and provided a cool, sheltered spot to sleep and work. Their beds were made of palm strips (*khafas*), while a rudimentary bookcase was created from planks of wood and Huntley and Palmers biscuit tins from Reading. In later recollections, Carter would reflect on his preference for tombs over tents as suitable accommodation and, indeed, tombs were regularly used in later archaeological projects.

Despite his youth, Carter's career in Egypt began positively. Newberry wrote to Griffith saying:[5]

> Our time (Carter's & my own) has been spent from morning till sunset entirely on tracing & we have now only a very little more to do here. I never reckoned on getting done so fast. It is astonishing how much can be done by two men working hard when the hands are willing. I believe that Carter & I could almost trace all the tombs in Egypt in five years!!!

13 *The east wall of the rock-cut tomb chapel of Khnumhotep II at Beni Hasan (tomb 3). The central niche once contained an engaged statue of the deceased framed by scenes of him fishing and fowling. Image by author.*

The ambitious pace of work continued, but fractures in the Survey team were clearly forming. Newberry's reference to 'willing' hands may imply that Fraser and Blackden were no longer as dedicated to the task.

As 'tracer' for the Survey, Carter was responsible for recording the decorated wall scenes in the tomb chapels. This meant covering the walls in tracing paper and copying the scenes like for like. The subsequent publication of the scenes by the EEF remain some of the most important of their kind because of this faithful representation. However, when compared with Carter's skills as

14 *A line drawing published as plate 34 in* Beni Hasan I *showing the eastern wall of the tomb-chapel of Khnumhotep II. The interior of the figures and hieroglyphs have been block-coloured in black. This is in contrast with Carter and Blackden's watercolours which give a better sense of the colour preserved in the tombs. Courtesy of the Egypt Exploration Society.*

an artist, it is clear that there was much room for improvement in these early methods. Carter himself would later lament:[6]

> I was disappointed to find that the *modus operandi* was to hang large sheets of tracing paper on the walls and with a soft pencil trace the scenes upon them, no matter whether the scenes were painted in the flat, sculptures in relief, or the wall surfaces were smooth or granular. Such completed tracings were then rolled up and sent to England, where they would be inked in with a brush, and all inside the outlines of the figures filled in black like a silhouette, more often than not by persons without any knowledge of the original or of drawing. […]

The detailed records created by Carter showing individual hieroglyphs and scenes testify to the detail missing in the final published line drawings. Carter's technique was to present the scene as he saw it, blurring areas that were damaged or unclear. His colleagues, notably Blackden, instead chose to complete the scenes, restoring them on paper to, what they believed to be, their original condition. Carter would come to perfect his technique which would become the standard for epigraphic recording moving forward. The paintings are, even today, a useful record for understanding the condition of the scenes recorded over time. It is possible to note whether the scenes have deteriorated through exposure to sunlight or malicious damage – albeit with an understanding that this was Carter's impression and not a scientific record.

Carter's skills would be rewarded when he was later employed to ink the drawings for publication himself in the UK. This both extended his employment, as well as enabling him to pioneer his new standards for reproduction which can be seen in the later publications of the Archaeological Survey of Egypt.

Carter's future as an archaeologist, rather than an artist, took a dramatic turn in late 1891 with the controversial discovery of the alabaster quarries of Hatnub.

Howard Carter: from Tracer to Tutankhamun

15 Top, a cat in papyrus marshes, Howard Carter, 1891 (EES.ART.230). Left, a sacred ibis in the papyrus marshes, Howard Carter, 1891 (EES.ART.231). Both as depicted on the eastern wall of the tomb-chapel of Khnumhotep II and visible in figure 14. Note Carter's initials at the bottom of each painting. Courtesy of the Egypt Exploration Society.

Carl Graves

16 *Above, a hoopoe bird in an acacia tree as depicted on the east wall of the tomb-chapel of Khnumhotep II at Beni Hasan, Howard Carter (EES.ART.211). Below, the same scene published as plate 33 in* Beni Hasan I *– the hoopoe bird is in the lower left of the bird-catching scene. Courtesy of the Egypt Exploration Society.*

17 *Three bird hieroglyphs painted by Howard Carter in 1891 (top to bottom: EES.ART.004, 006 and 022). Courtesy of the Egypt Exploration Society.*

18 *Plate 2, Beni Hasan III. The three birds in figure 17 can be seen alongside other examples by Carter and others by Marcus W Blackden. The different artists can be discerned by the clean lines and complete examples by Blackden (see those in each corner of the plate) and Carter's depiction of the damaged or unclear parts of each sign. Courtesy of the Egypt Exploration Society.*

19 *Birds in an acacia tree as depicted on the east wall of the tomb-chapel of Khnumhotep II at Beni Hasan, by Marcus Blackden (EES.ART.218). This scene is missing in figure 16 showing Khnumhotep II netting birds. Courtesy of the Egypt Exploration Society.*

20 Plate 25 from El Bersheh I. *An example of a later line drawing published by Carter showing his changing style, including the depiction of damaged areas and lack of in-filling individual figures. Courtesy of the Egypt Exploration Society.*

Scandals in the sand: The case of 'Boot and Barefoot'

Hatnub (ḥwt-nbw, Mansion of Gold) is an area of Egyptian alabaster (also called travertine) quarries roughly 20km south of the ancient city of Amarna in the eastern desert. It is just east of the great stone outcrop of Abu Feda which runs up to the Nile in this area of Middle Egypt, creating a largely uninhabited section of the ancient valley and was, therefore, somewhat remote during the Pharaonic Period. The tale of its discovery betrays the fragile balance in the team of the Archaeological Survey of Egypt during 1891 and the competitiveness of those working in Egypt at the time.

In November 1891, the Archaeological Survey of Egypt team relocated from Beni Hasan to the tomb-chapels of Deir el-Bersha, a little to the south. These tombs were similar in date and construction to those at Beni Hasan and were within the Middle

Egyptian area targeted by the Survey (see figure 9). On 19th December 1891, Newberry and Carter left Deir el-Bersha to visit W M F Petrie at Amarna for a few days, 10 km to the south. The proximity of the two sites meant that, though Petrie was excavating independently from the EEF, the two British teams remained in regular contact. Newberry and Carter used the opportunity of visiting to explore the surrounding desert area to map inscriptions, graffiti, and quarries. In one such excursion from Beni Hasan to Antinoopolis, Newberry reported to Amelia Edwards that he and Carter had nothing but 'bread, water, and onions (!)' to sustain them.[7] However, Newberry had ulterior motives; he was also on the lookout for the rumoured tomb of the 18th Dynasty Pharaoh, Akhenaten. It was already known that Amarna was the ancient site of Akhetaten (Horizon of the Aten), the short-lived capital of Egypt founded by Akhenaten, the probable father of Tutankhamun (born Tutankhaten). It was here that worship of the Aten, the deified sun-disk, was promoted above other deities in the Egyptian pantheon, and where Akhenaten relocated his royal court. Tutankhamun, the son of a lesser wife of Akhenaten, was likely born and raised here and where he began his reign before restoring the traditional pantheon and returning the royal court to the administrative centres of Memphis and Thebes.

On 21st December, Newberry, Petrie, and Carter approached a Bedouin camp in the eastern desert and one man, Sheikh Eid, described a feature that matched what they were searching for. Suspecting the lost tomb of Akhenaten, Shiekh Eid agreed to take them there on his camels and they set off the next day into the desert.[8]

Newberry reported what they discovered back to Griffith from their camp at Deir el-Bersha on 23rd December:[9]

> After about 3 ½ more hours we at last came in sight of great heaps of limestone chips. You may judge of our excitement when we got quite close to them – and of our disappointment when we found it was only an alabaster quarry!

Later in the letter, Newberry reports finding the cartouches of Khufu (4th Dynasty) and Merenre (6th Dynasty) during their brief investigation of the quarries. He then pondered, '? Is this the alabaster quarry which Una [Weni] worked; from this royal name it is not unlikely.' Here, Newberry is referring to the 6th Dynasty autobiographical inscription of Weni who was sent on an expedition to Hatnub in order to bring an alabaster altar for use in the pyramid complex of the King:[10]

> His majesty sent me to Hatnub to bring a great altar of alabaster of Hatnub. I brought this altar down for him in seventeen days. After it was quarried at Hatnub, I had it go downstream in this barge I had built for it, a barge of acacia wood of sixty cubits in length and thirty cubits in width. Assembled in seventeen days, in the third month of summer, when there was no water on the sandbanks, it landed at the pyramid "Merenre-appears-in-splendour" in safety. It came about through me entirely in accordance with the ordinance commanded by my lord.

Newberry and Carter must have related news of their discovery to Fraser and Blackden over Christmas, but feelings in the Survey team had already turned sour. Newberry's letter to Griffith (above) noted that both Fraser and Blackden would spend Christmas day with Newberry at Major Brown's in Minia, to which he vented: 'If I had known they were going I most certainly would not have accepted as they both have made it most abominably uncomfortable for me here – but I will tell you more of this when I come home.'

Petrie, though working independently of the Fund at this time, reported how the quarries of Hatnub were discovered. His published account gives some indication of the grievances about to occur:[11]

> This quarry was first visited by Mr. Newberry, guided there by the Arabs last year; and the inscriptions in it prove it to be the

celebrated quarry of Hatnub, from whence Una obtained the alabaster altar for the pyramid of Mehtiemsaf. It seems also, by the name of Khufu, to have been the source of the great blocks of alabaster in the granite temple at Gizeh. All the inscriptions have now been copied by Messrs. Blackden and Fraser.

After Christmas, on 27th December 1891, Fraser and Blackden left the camp to spend three days away, unbeknownst to Newberry, recording the inscriptions at the quarry. From an analysis of the inscriptions, they confirmed that it was, indeed, the quarries of Hatnub referred to in the inscriptions.

Hatnub was a name already known to the Archaeological Survey of Egypt team as its name was recorded in the tomb chapel of Djehutyhotep at Deir el-Bersha which the team were already busy copying. Carter himself was tasked with tracing the famous scene showing a colossal statue of Djehutyhotep being dragged by two hundred men. The long inscription behind the colossus says:[12]

> Following the statue of 13 cubits [c. 7m tall, weighing c. 58 tonnes] in stone of Hatnub. Behold, very wonderful was the road upon which it came. Behold, wonderful was the dragging of valuable stone along it on account of the rocky way from the quarry, and difficult would it have been even for a mere square block of sandstone. I caused to come troops of goodly youths in order to move it, together with tomb-sculptors and quarrymen, the foremen knowing how to point out the strong-armed. The townsmen all rejoiced at its arrival: it was better to see than anything. Behold, this well carved statue was more costly than anything.

Around the scene are captions explaining the activities Carter recorded. The man on top of the statue says: 'Giving the time-beat to the soldiers by the signal-giver (crying) "Djehutihetep! Beloved of the king!"' Either for ritual purposes or to lubricate the path for moving it, water is poured in front of the colossus.

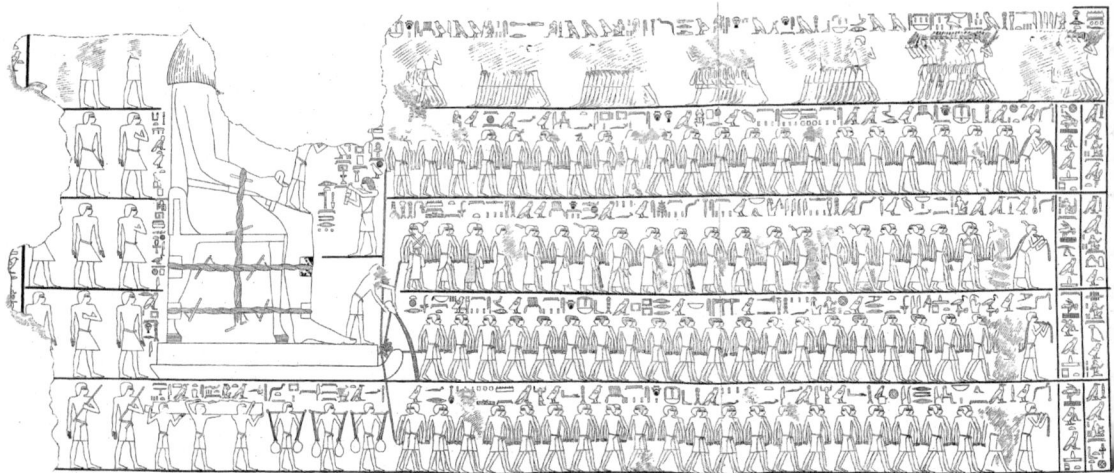

21 *Plate 15 from* El Bersheh I *showing the colossal statue of Djehutyhotep being dragged from the quarries of Hatnub. Courtesy of the Egypt Exploration Society.*

Beneath are men carrying water and it tells us this with the caption: 'Carrying water by men of the house of eternity', that is, people employed to maintain the funerary cult of Djehuty-hotep after his death.

A letter, written by Petrie, gives a more unusual account of events than his published report. The letter, copied by EEF Secretary Emily Paterson and now in the EES archives, records a strange incident he calls 'the mystery of Boot and Barefoot' in which Blackden and Fraser actively tried to forestall Newberry and Carter:[13]

> I sighted a print of a boot in the sand, and a boot in an out-of-the-way desert is as much as the footprint to Robinson Crusoe. There was a wild hope that it was some official going to look after the tomb of Khuenaten [Akhenaten]; for that, and Tutankhamun's, have been known to all the museums for two years past, and are now being kept in reserve by Grébaut to float his reputation at the last gasp. We anxiously tracked "Boot" who was accompanied by a native "Barefoot", up and down little ravines. Boot went in

22 *Plate 14 from* El Bersheh I *showing the long inscription referring to the moving of the colossus of Djehutyhotep. Courtesy of the Egypt Exploration Society.*

> the most headlong way, and after a couple of miles or so came some confusion, and Boot struck away from the mountain. I hunted closer and found that Barefoot had led Boot up to see a natural pit in the rock produced by water action, which would never have been adopted for a tomb. Then Boot went down and soon mounted a donkey that was waiting for him, joined a camel and so returned.
>
> Carter has come over, and the mystery of "Boot and Barefoot" is out. It was Fraser and Blackden, intent on forestalling Newberry. Having heard all Newberry had to say, they rushed over, and began searching for Khuenaten's tomb. They kept away in the desert for three days that we should not know about it, but the Arabs told Newberry of the matter and they had to agree to the whole story boots and all. Fraser and Blackden came over with two camels, servant on donkey, and a guide. The affair does not leave a pleasant taste in the mouth.

Newberry was angered by the subversions of Fraser and Blackden and considered it unscholarly to have claimed the discovery of Hatnub for themselves when, in fact, it was himself and Carter who had made the discovery. By January 1892, Newberry was so incensed that he tendered his resignation from the Archaeological Survey, writing to Amelia Edwards on 4th January saying:

> I very much regret to have to inform you that circumstances have arisen which compel me to resign my post on the staff of the Archaeological Survey of Egypt. […] I fear that it will be impossible for me to undertake any further work out here.[14]

His resignation was read at a meeting of the EEF Committee on 7th March 1892 and accepted, though withdrawn at a later meeting on 27th May that year following further correspondence from Newberry.

Newberry continued to run the Archaeological Survey after a brief hiatus in work, but Fraser and Blackden's roles were

23 A copy of Newberry's resignation letter in the EES Archives transcribed by Emily Paterson, Assistant Secretary to Amelia Edwards. EES.COR.017.d.22-1. Courtesy of the Egypt Exploration Society.

terminated and their very promising careers at the Survey cut short. In 1894, following further visits to the quarries, Fraser and Blackden published the inscriptions that they recorded at Hatnub. The provocative title, *Collection of Hieratic Graffiti, from the Alabaster Quarry of Hat-nub, situated near Tell el Amarna. Found December 28th, 1891, copied September, 1892. By M. W. Blackden and G. Willoughby Fraser, F.S.A.* did little to mend bridges with the Survey by giving the discovery date of 28th December, despite Newberry and Carter visiting on 22nd December. The true 'discoverers', the Bedouins (including Sheikh Eid) who showed Newberry and Carter to the quarries, remain nameless and unacknowledged in the published reports. In 1895, further inscriptions from the quarries were published by Newberry with translations by Griffith in *Deir el-Bersha* of the Archaeological

Survey of Egypt series. More than 50 inscriptions have been discovered around the quarries of Hatnub. Many of these are carved but the majority are simply painted, often using a red pigment. These were left by those sent to quarry the rock at Hatnub and date predominantly from the Old to Middle Kingdoms, with a few outliers.

The site continues to be an area of archaeological investigation where modern imaging techniques have revealed even more graffiti and inscriptions.

In hindsight, the somewhat petty instance of 'Boot and Barefoot', had far reaching implications for the young Howard Carter who became caught up in the affair. Before the conflict arose between the team, Blackden had been selected for further archaeological training by Petrie at Amarna in 1892. However, because of the now irretrievable situation, Blackden's training opportunity was revoked, and another trainee was required. Carter found himself in a good position; not only could Petrie take him on, but the Amhersts were also keen to offer a financial incentive to Petrie, in return for a share of the artefacts discovered.

Carter arrived at Amarna on 2nd January 1892 and Petrie recorded: 'Mr Carter came here and settled in, building a room and roofing it with boards and durra-stalks like mine. His position here is to be as agent for Mr Tyssen Amherst. […] Mr Carter is a good-natured lad, whose interest is entirely in painting and natural history; he only takes this digging as being on the spot and convenient to Mr Amherst and it is of no use for me to work him up as an excavator.'[15] Though this statement may seem short-sighted, by this time, Carter had only a few months experience in Egypt. Carter would, himself, write in 1893 to Griffith: 'Please to remember that I am an artist & cannot see what way digging for antiquities should advance me in my future career.'[16] On the other hand, Petrie would report to the EEF Committee on 3rd January in that same year, in relation to his views on Édouard Naville's (1844–1926) skills as an archaeologist:[17]

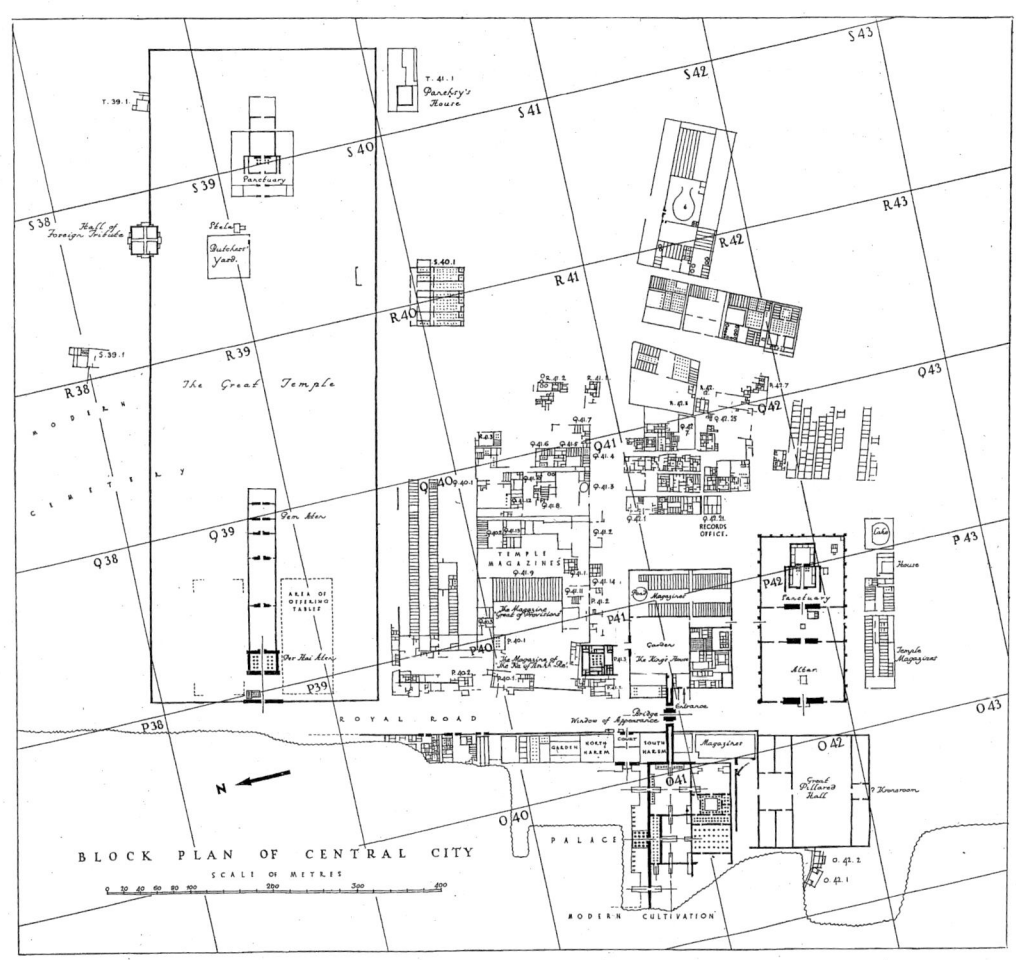

24 *Plan of the Central City of Akhetaten (Amarna). The Great Aten Temple is in the rectangular enclosure on the left (north) of the image. Plate 1 of* City of Akhetaten III. *Courtesy of the Egypt Exploration Society.*

> The most competent man you can employ to excavate, at the time, is I believe M. Carter. He understands what he sees; but he has not the general education for the best work in excavating.

On arriving at Amarna, Carter received a week of instruction from Petrie before issuing him the task of excavating the Great Aten Temple and managing a team of Egyptian excavators to complete the work. The temple area is 240,000 m² and remains an area of active archaeological excavation even today. The pressure of the work and responsibility almost killed Carter and various travellers reported seeing him on the brink of illness, some even offering to feed him or prescribing medical treatments. Carter's finds from the Great Aten Temple area were subsequently distributed to Lord Amherst in return for his financing of the excavations. This included some fine fragments of statuary which were eventually sold at Sotheby's and acquired, largely, by the Metropolitan Museum of Art in New York.

It was during this season of work at Amarna that Carter's father passed away, as well as Petrie's mother, and Amelia Edwards. The two men may have bonded over this shared grief, though neither were prepared to note down their shared sorrow. When Carter finally returned to England at the end of May 1892,

25 *Upper torso of Nefertiti discovered during Carter's work at Amarna in 1892. The Queen's body is engraved with the early cartouches of the Aten, while she wears a thin pleated garment pulled over her left shoulder. MMA 21.9.4.*

26 *Goat herders from the tomb of Djehutyhotep at Deir el-Bersha, see figure 20 for line drawing. EES.ART.213. Courtesy of the Egypt Exploration Society.*

he had embarked on a career as an archaeological epigrapher and excavator at the age of just 18.

Carter continued his work for Newberry by inking drawings back in England ready for publication and recording the scenes at Deir el-Bersha and, later, El-Sheikh Said. In 1893, Carter introduced a new method for copying the decoration in the tomb-chapels at the latter:[18]

> I introduced a new and what I thought a far better method. In place of the tracing paper, to employ a suitable tough white linen paper, and by the application of light pressure, by carefully pressing the paper with the finger and thumb on the reliefs, thus obtain an impression, a sort of dry squeeze, sufficient for the purpose of guiding the eye and hand, while making full-sized completed copies in pencil direct from the originals.

In December 1893, Carter was taken on by Édouard Naville (1844–1926) at the EEF excavations of Deir el-Bahari. The mortuary temple of the 18th Dynasty Pharaoh Hatshepsut had been previously recorded by Auguste Mariette, for the Service des Antiquités, but much remained to be cleared and recorded. Carter joined Naville as a deputy and was given the mammoth task of

27 *The mortuary temple of Hatshepsut at Deir el-Bahari where Carter worked for the EEF under the direction of Édouard Naville from 1894-99. Image by author.*

recording the temple scenes in watercolour and photography as well as reconstructing the fallen masonry wherever possible. By now, Carter's experience in recording as well as excavating and managing an Egyptian team made him ideal for the work. Naville also gave Carter a freehand in developing new systems for recording the scenes preserved in the temple. Carter wrote:[19]

> I felt that if I attempted to copy the scenes sculptured upon the walls of Hatshepsut's mortuary temple by the prevailing system of tracing, the essential charm of these beautiful reliefs would have vanished in my copy. And as Professor Naville had given me free hand in the matter, I felt bounden to study the problem, to find a means to attain the best results. I tried many expedients; but they resolved in the simple solution: to first observe the fundamental laws of Egyptian art; how it eliminates the unessentials; to copy that art accurately and intelligently with honest work, a free hand, a good pencil, and suitable paper.

Howard Carter: from Tracer to Tutankhamun

28 *Howard Carter (standing left) with a team of Egyptian excavators by a carriage of the Decauville Railway used to clear the temple of Deir el-Bahari. EES.DB-HAT.NEG.C.01. Courtesy of the Egypt Exploration Society.*

29 *Howard Carter moving a stone Hathoric capital into the Hathor sanctuary of the temple of Hatshepsut at Deir el-Bahari. As well as photographer and epigrapher, Carter was also responsible for reconstructing elements of the temple resulting in the edifice seen by visitors today. Somers Clarke, an architect and archaeologist (1841–1926) said of Carter's reconstruction: 'I cannot speak too highly of Mr Carter and the resources he has shewn in bringing the work toward a new conclusion without any accident.' EES.DB-HAT.NEG.04.40: Courtesy of the Egypt Exploration Society.*

30 *A photograph, taken by Howard Carter, showing the rear wall of the upper shrine of Anubis. The niche, from which EEA.ART.224 is drawn, opens to the left of the image. On a copy of this photograph now in the Peggy Joy Egyptology Library, Howard's sister Amy Joyce wrote, 'This photo was taken by flash light by Howard Carter. The small articles in the foreground are some of his appliances'. To the right, propped against the wall, is probably Carter's drawing board – perhaps the same used to create EES.ART.224. EES. DB-HAT.NEG.C.39: Courtesy of the Egypt Exploration Society.*

31 Left, the profile of Queen Ahmose as depicted at the temple of Hatshepsut at Deir el-Bahari as copied by Carter in 1896. Naville considered the Queen's depiction to be 'perhaps the finest piece of work in the whole temple'. EES.ART.221. Right, the same scene in photographic form. EES.DB-HAT.NEG.C.42. Courtesy of the Egypt Exploration Society.

The exact methods used by Carter to create the records found in archives today remains somewhat of a mystery. Biographers and epigraphers have not easily been able to deduce the techniques – whether by initial tracings, dry squeezes, or use of a camera lucida – that Carter used, though it is clear that he developed his techniques over time and for different situations. Carter's biographer, T G H James concluded that, at Deir el-Bahari, Carter drew the scenes free hand on good quality heavy cartridge paper after outlining, faintly in a hard pencil, some guidelines based on existing decoration. Then, by eye and a skilled hand he drew the rest of the scene to scale set up by the paper and guidelines. James deduced that Carter did complete his drawings in front of the scene before it was checked by Naville prior to submission for printers. Whatever the exact method, Carter's ability to complete such a mammoth task while also training others confuses the matter further. Through training, Carter was assisted in the copying of the temple scenes by assistants. One of these was his own brother, Vernet (Verney) Carter. Howard's methods were replicated so faithfully that it is sometimes difficult to distinguish between the work of the brothers where they have not signed their work. Vernet only joined Howard for one season in 1894, however, as the hot Egyptian climate was not to his liking. Similarly, the work of Rosalind Paget (1844–1925, who joined the team in 1895–97), captured the lively and colourful scenes, some showing Hatshepsut's expedition to the land of Punt, before they faded from exposure to wind-blown sands and sunlight.[20]

32 *Nekhbet vulture from the hall of the chapel of Anubis at Deir el-Bahari, by Vernet Carter, 1894. Watercolours and Drawings 202&203. Copyright Griffith Institute, University of Oxford.*

Carl Graves

33 *Vernet Carter in 1894 at Deir el-Bahari during the one season he assisted his brother in copying the scenes. He did not return as he could not handle the heat of Egypt. EES.DB-HAT.NEG.C.64. Courtesy of the Egypt Exploration Society.*

Hatshepsut ruled Egypt during the 18th Dynasty and drew her legitimation to rule from her descendance from her father, Tuthmosis I. Her husband, Tuthmosis II, was also her half-brother and son of Tuthmosis I. She spent much energy during her reign in honouring her father and ancestry and it can be seen in the decorative scheme of her temple at Deir el-Bahari too. EES. ART.224 is a full-scale reproduction of a scene from the upper shrine of Anubis (called the 'Chapel of Thothmes I' in reports by Naville) which opens off the north wall of the solar court (or Great Altar Court in Naville's reports) on the upper terrace of the temple of Hatshepsut. The specific scene is of the north wall of the internal niche within the shrine and, therefore, in a relatively protected area from natural elements that might have damaged it. It shows Tuthmosis I and his mother Senseneb before an offering table laden with food dedicated to the god

Anubis, a jackal-headed god of embalming, which is now missing (damaged) to the left. Very little is known about Senseneb, and this scene represents one of the few known depictions of her. She may have been of royal descent and thus her relationship to Tuthmosis I helped to legitimise his own rule.[21] EES.ART.224 is the largest known original watercolour by Howard Carter but is actually comprised of six pieces of paper compiled together to create this final scene. Pin pricks in the paper reveal how Carter attached the separate sheets of paper to a drawing board in order to work in front of the original scene. Opposite the relief is a similar subject, this time showing Hatshepsut and her mother, Queen Ahmose, making offerings to Amun-Re, the chief deity of the Egyptian pantheon at the time.

34 *Watercolour painting by Rosalind Paget showing detail from the scenes of Hatshepsut's expedition to Punt at Deir el-Bahari. EES.ART.219. Courtesy of the Egypt Exploration Society.*

During conservation work in 2022, the painting was cleaned and reframed. The back of the artwork showed that Carter used six irregular shaped pieces of paper following the contours of the figures. He was presumably limited by the paper sizes available to him and the practicality of using smaller pieces to work with on-site. He signed many of the separate pieces on the reverse but placed one prominent autograph on the front once compiled. This final autograph appears

35a *The largest original painting by Howard Carter, from the upper shrine of Anubis at Deir el-Bahari. EES.ART.224. Courtesy of the Egypt Exploration Society.*

35b *A modern line drawing of the watercolour. Artwork by Aakheperure MMXXIV. Courtesy of the Egypt Exploration Society.*

to be painted over an earlier signature. Carter dated the finished piece, 'March 1894'. In the final publication, the scene was reproduced in three different sections and not as a single piece, owing to its large scale.

36 *Plate 16 in* Deir el-Bahari I, *showing the scene from the southern wall of the niche in the upper shrine of Anubis and the damage made to the representation of Hatshepsut and, probably later, Amun-Re. Courtesy of the Egypt Exploration Society.*

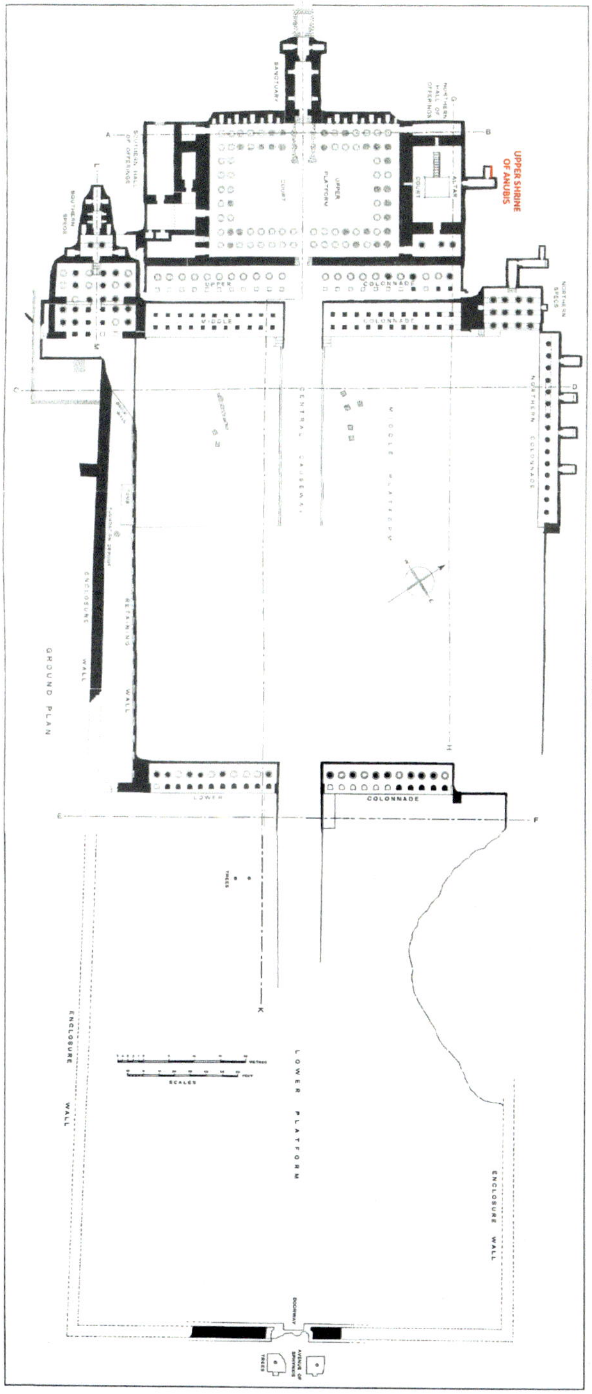

Howard Carter: from Tracer to Tutankhamun

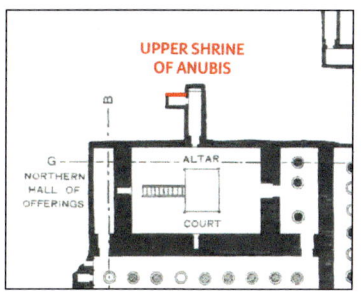

37 *Plan of the temple of Hatshepsut at Deir el-Bahari showing the location of the scene painted in EES.ART.224. Plate 172 in* Deir el-Bahari VI. *Courtesy of the Egypt Exploration Society.*

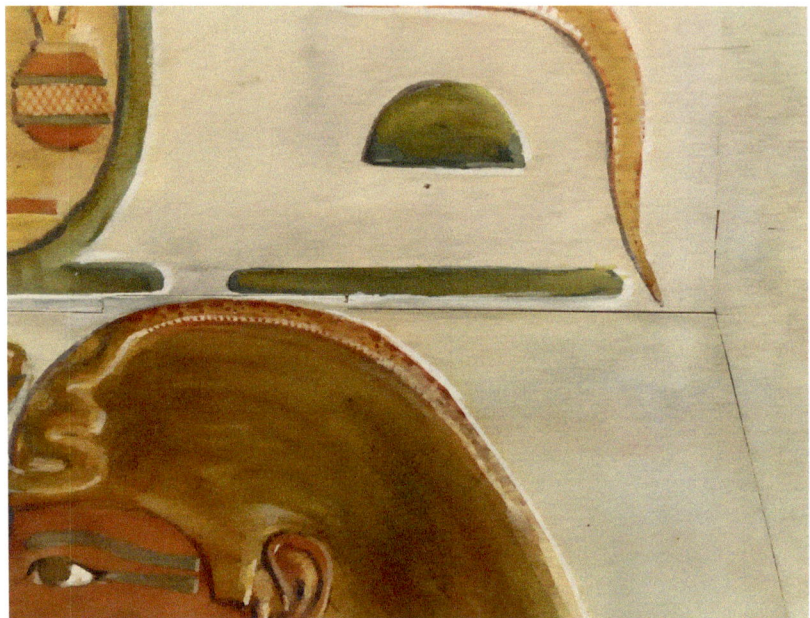

38 Detail of EES.ART.224 showing evidence of pins used to hold the paper to a drawing board (beneath the semi-circular hieroglyph [bread, t]) as well as the irregular cutting of the paper around the nemes headdress of the Pharaoh. Courtesy of the Egypt Exploration Society.

39 Detail of Howard Carter's signature on the bottom right of EES.ART.224. He has signed the painting over an older version which is only faintly discernible today. Courtesy of the Egypt Exploration Society.

40 *Carter, on the far left, with [1] Percy Newberry, [2] Édouard Naville, [3 – missing] Abdul Maleik (servant), [4] Said Gaddis (cook), and [5] Shehâté (scribe). Copyright Peggy Joy Egyptology Library.*

The Inspector, 1901–1905

Carter's reputation in archaeology had risen fast and, in October 1899, the French-run Service des Antiquités de l'Égypte appointed two new inspectors – both British. This was an important moment in Anglo-Franco relations in Egyptian archaeology and had long been sought by British organisations such as the Society for the Preservation of the Monuments of Ancient Egypt and the EEF. Naville recommended Carter for the position to Gaston Maspero, Director of the Service. This, of course, meant losing Carter from Deir el-Bahari but would place a British scholar (and EEF contact) directly in the Service des Antiquités. Carter was offered the role and became Chief Inspector of Antiquities for Upper Egypt, while James Edward Quibell (1867–1935) would become Chief Inspector for Lower Egypt.

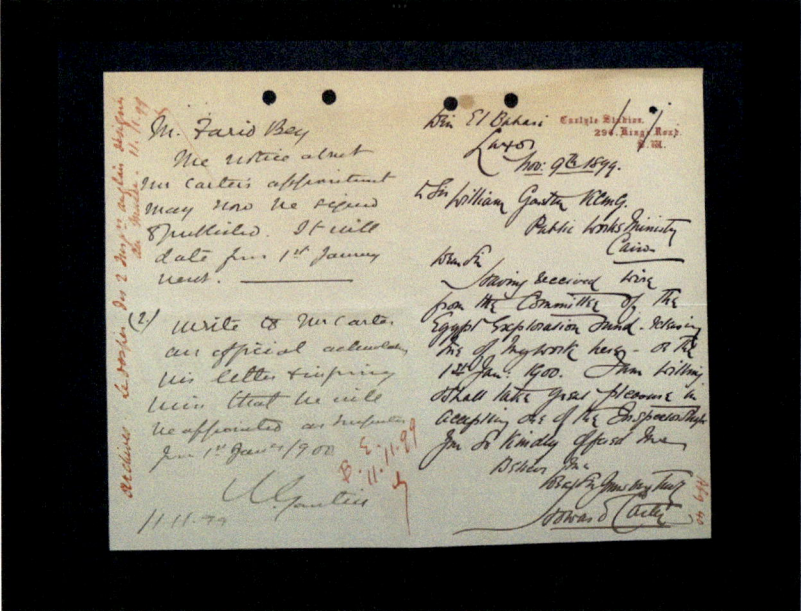

41 *Carter's letter to William Garstin (1849-1925, Under Secretary of State for Public Works in Egypt) accepting the role of Inspector of Antiquities in Upper Egypt from 1st January 1900. Copyright Tony Marks.*

On Carter's appointment, Maspero wrote:[22]

> I have been at Luxor since 26 December and I have installed Carter. […] I find him very active, a very good young man, a little obstinate, but I believe that things will go well when he is persuaded of the impossibility of securing all the reforms in one go: the only misfortune is that he doesn't understand French.

As Chief Inspector for Upper Egypt, Carter was given a home near to Medinet Habu and the Colossi of Memnon on the west bank of Luxor – often called 'Castle Carter', by Carter himself. This building still stands today near to the ticket office. Carter turned this home into a menagerie, perhaps reminiscent of his childhood memories of farmsteads and his cottage upbringing in Norfolk. Over the course of his residence, he shared his

42 *Carter at his new home near Medinet Habu ('Castle Carter') with his horse, Sultan. One of Carter's pet gazelles is climbing up on Mr Cole. The identity of the Egyptian man on the right is unknown. Copyright Peggy Joy Egyptology Library.*

house with his horse, Sultan, two gazelles and a donkey, called San-Toy. Though Carter loved animals and drawing them, he was not wholly successful in keeping them alive. Sadly, both gazelles and San-Toy[23] died in unfortunate circumstances, the latter being bitten in the mouth by a cobra.

Within a month of his appointment Carter, surprisingly, returned to Deir el-Bahari. His reason for this was to clear up something that had, literally, stumbled him two years earlier. Back in November 1898, when working for the EEF, Carter's horse, Sultan, had tripped in the desert sand revealing a small hole. This area, at the time, lay outside the EEF concession and so they were unable to investigate further. Now, in 1900, Carter had the opportunity to revisit this potential discovery and began excavating. Today, this feature is known as Bab el-Hosan, or Gate/Tomb of the Horse.

The excavations revealed a 17 m long passageway ending in an intact blocked entrance. Beyond this, the team cleared a 150 m long tunnel reaching a chamber. Within the chamber lay a wooden coffin and a large, sandstone statue wrapped in linen. This regally proportioned statue was uninscribed, and its identity remained a mystery. A vertical shaft in the floor promised further reward and Carter's team spent almost the whole year clearing it to a depth of 30 m. There, at the bottom, a chamber containing just three wooden boats and some pots was all that was to be found. However, Carter had made an error of judgement in his new discovery. He had notified Lord Cromer, British Consul-General in Egypt, that an intact royal burial was to be found. With great pageantry, Cromer arrived in Luxor to see the discovery firsthand only to the embarrassment of Carter when no burial was found and only wooden models and ceramic pots could be presented. There is little surprise that Carter would check his findings before notifying press and diplomats in the future.

43 *Statue of Mentuhotep Nebhepetre wearing the red crown (deshret) of Lower Egypt and* heb-sed *festival robes, found in Bab el-Hosan by Carter's team in 1900. Today it is on display in the Egyptian Museum, Cairo (JE36195). Image by author, courtesy of the Egyptian Museum Cairo.*

In 1904, the EEF continued their investigations at Deir el-Bahari by excavating the area to the south of Hatshepsut's temple. Eventually, they would uncover the mortuary temple of Mentuhotep Nebhepetre, founder of the Middle Kingdom, and the tombs of his royal family. Bab el-Hosan was located within this wider enclosure and thus the identity of the statue uncovered there was revealed.

Carter continued to maintain his relationship with the Amhersts and returned the favours they had bestowed on him. In 1901, when Lady William Cecil, daughter of the Amhersts, was visiting Aswan, Carter joined her and visited the tombs of Qubbet el-Hawa discovered by Francis Grenfell in 1885. Lady William ventured that there would be more tombs to find, and Carter agreed to get her a permit to excavate. It is probable that Carter acted as a teacher in this stage before Lady William undertook her own arrangements, furnishing museums with new artefacts. Her excavations were well published in the antiquities journals of the time and she was applauded by Maspero for her careful investigation. Today, these tombs are commonly known as the 'Cecil Tombs'. In that same year, Carter was also responsible for foiling the robbery of the tomb of Amenhotep II (KV35) in the Valley of the Kings. The mummied body of the king was damaged, but Carter succeeded in bringing Mohamed Abd er-Rasul to court based on his forensic recording of footprints found at the scene of the crime. No charges were made and Carter was unable to retrieve a wooden model boat stolen from the tomb. Many years later, Carter would identify the boat on display in the Egyptian Museum having been purchased from an antiquities trader who had purchased it from Mohamed Abd er-Rasul. This episode added to Carter's in-depth knowledge of the antiquities trade in Egypt which would serve him in later dealings with museums and collectors.

From 1900, Carter was working in the Valley of the Kings, the ancient burial ground for Egypt's New Kingdom royals. In his role as Chief Inspector, he helped to secure the known tombs

44 *The Qubbet el-Hawa on the west bank of Aswan where Carter secured permission for Lady William Cecil to excavate in 1901. Image by author.*

by installing iron gates and managing security. Some investigations required more supervision than others, such as the excavations of Chinouda Macarios and Boutros Andraos, two privately funded individuals. Under Carter's supervision, they discovered and excavated KV42. The layout of the tomb is of an early 18th Dynasty royal style, turning 90 degrees with a cartouche shaped burial chamber. In it, Carter found traces of the burial of queen Hatshepsut-Meryetre, including two previously unknown foundation deposits in the chamber indicating that she was the original owner. Hatshepsut-Meryetre was a wife of Tuthmosis III (buried in KV34) and mother of Amenhotep II and was ultimately buried in her son's tomb with KV42 being passed onto the Sennefer family by royal gift.

By 1902, Carter had persuaded the American lawyer Theodore Davis (1838–1915) to fund excavations in the Valley. This time, Carter was supervising the excavations himself on behalf of

Davis and began systematically clearing parts of the main Valley and a side-wadi. In early 1903, Carter found foundation deposits including the inscribed name of Tuthmosis IV before revealing the entrance high up the cliff face. On 18 January 1903, Carter entered the tomb with Davis' friend, Robb de Peyster Tytus who was working with Newberry at the nearby palace of Amenhotep III (Malqata) at the time.

The tomb of Tuthmosis IV (KV43) is typical of the Tuthmoside Period. Its layout turns back on itself with two 90-degree angles in the descent to the burial chamber. A deep shaft is one of the first elements reached and was perhaps intended to deter tomb robbers or protect the burial from the surging flood waters which are known to affect the Valley of the Kings.

On reaching the shaft, Carter reported:[24]

> We looked down into dusty excavated space. At the edge of this abyss we waited until our eyes became more accustomed to the dim light of our candles, and then we realised in the gloom that the upper part of the walls of this well were elaborately

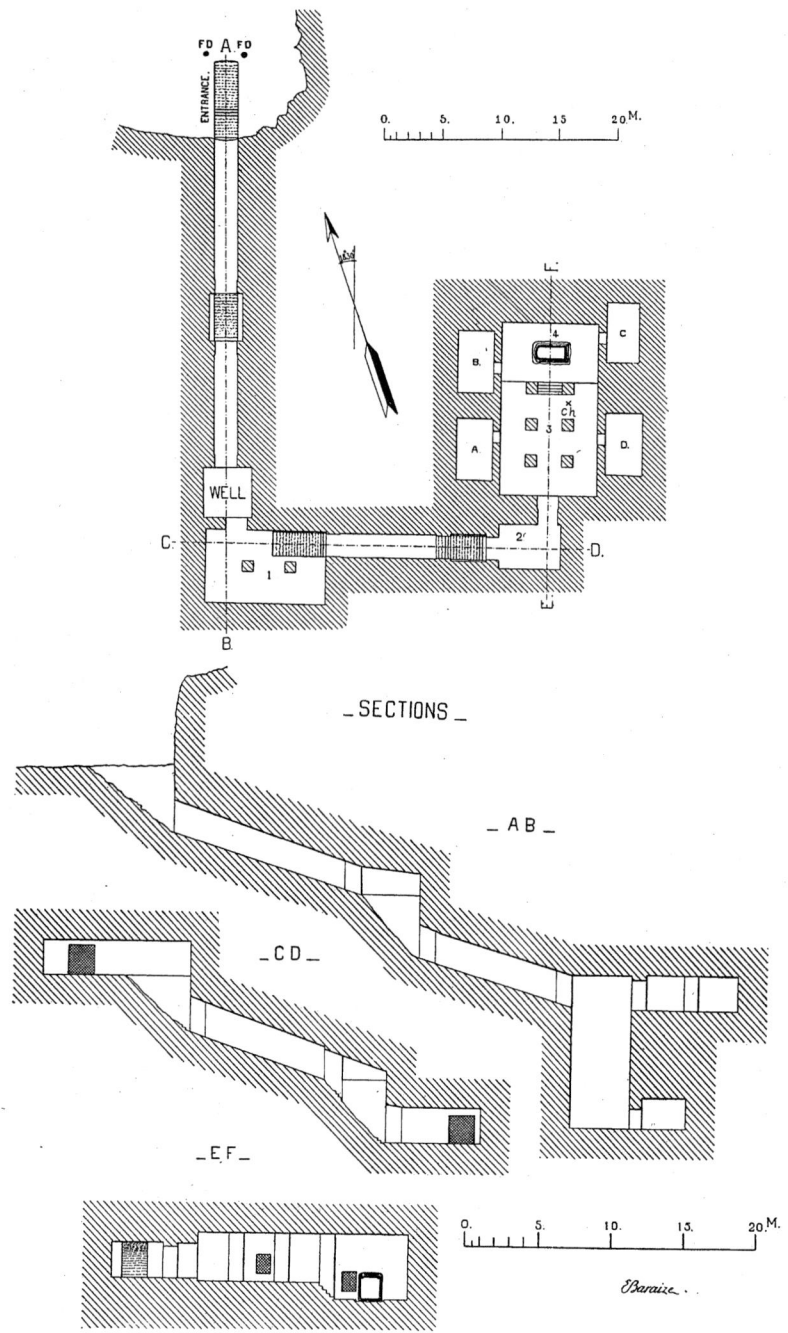

45 *Plan of the tomb of Tuthmosis IV (KV43), from* The Tomb of Thoutmôsis IV.

> sculptured and painted. The scenes represented the Pharaoh Tuthmosis IV standing before various gods and goddesses of the Netherworld. Each of these scenes was accompanied by explanatory inscriptions. Here was final proof that I had found the tomb of Tuthmosis IV, which, as you may conceive, gave me a considerable degree of satisfaction…

The tomb is notable for its bright decoration showing the king with various deities, but also for a restoration inscription dated to the reign of Horemheb at the end of the 18th Dynasty:[25]

> Year 8, third month of *akhet*, day one, under the majesty of the King of Upper and Lower Egypt, Djeserkheperure-setepenre, Son of Re, Horemheb-merenamun. His majesty (life, prosperity, and health) commanded that the fan-bearer on the king's right hand, the king's scribe, overseer of the treasury, overseer of the works in the Place of Eternity [royal necropolis] and leader of the festival of Amun in Karnak, Maya, son of the noble Iawy, born of the lady of the house Weret, be charged to renew the burial of king Menkheperure [Tuthmosis IV], true of voice, in the noble mansion upon the west of Thebes.

Following the Amarna Period, in which Akhenaten promoted the cult of the Aten, many of Egypt's earlier monuments fell into disuse and were exposed to looting. The restoration of Egypt's traditions under Tutankhamun, and continued under his successors Aye and Horemheb, are shown by this inscription of the latter's reign.

Though KV43 had been plundered in antiquity, the remains found by Carter gave him an idea of what an intact royal burial of the 18th Dynasty might contain. Most impressive among the artefacts was a chariot of the king showing him trampling enemies under the protection of the war-god Montu in a similar motif to those found on the lost wooden boat of Amenhotep II noted above.[26]

46 *Above and opposite page, the decoration of the chariot of Tuthmosis IV, from* The Tomb of Thoutmôsis IV.

Howard Carter: from Tracer to Tutankhamun

THE CHARIOT

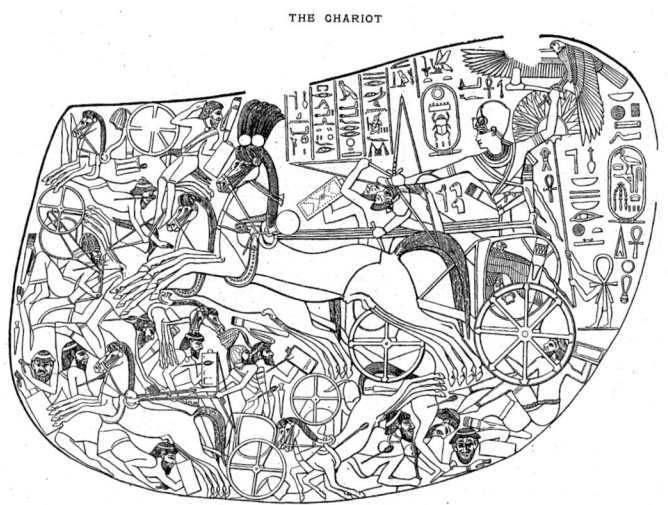

LEFT SIDE OF THE CHARIOT (EXTERIOR)

THE CHARIOT

LEFT SIDE OF THE CHARIOT (INTERIOR)

Carter continued his inspection of the side-wadi and noted that an earlier discovered tomb (KV20) was directly in line with the temple of Hatshepsut on the other side of the Theban hills. Sending a team to investigate, they uncovered two further foundation deposits, this time naming Hatshepsut herself. It took until 10th March 1904 to fully clear the tomb when they found, in the burial chamber, the empty sarcophagi of Hatshepsut and her father, Tuthmosis I. The body of Tuthmosis I had later been relocated by Tuthmosis III to a new tomb elsewhere in the Valley (KV38) before eventually being placed in the royal cache of DB320 at Deir el-Bahari cleared by Egyptologists in 1881.

Carter continued to work in the Valley, supervising the discovery and clearing of KV44 and KV45, both reused in the 22nd Dynasty. He also went on to discover a new tomb (later given the reference KV60) which was a simple corridor containing two burials. One of the bodies uncovered was identified as a wet nurse of Hatshepsut called Sitre In, known from a statue discovered at Deir el-Bahari. The second is now identified, by some, as Hatshepsut herself. However, as the burial was uninscribed, this was not known to Carter at the time.

In late 1904, Carter was relocated from Luxor to Cairo as a planned switch of the Inspectors of Upper and Lower Egypt. Carter lost the luxury of living in the Service house at Medinet Habu and his menagerie as he was forced to find his own accommodation in Cairo and cover the cost. Davis, on the other hand, would continue his financing of exploration in the Valley of the Kings largely under the direction of Quibell, Edward Ayrton (1882–1914) and Ernest Harold Jones (1877–1911).

47 *A shabti of Tuthmosis IV found in his tomb in 1903 and subsequently donated to the Metropolitan Museum of Art in New York. MMA 30.8.27.*

Howard Carter: from Tracer to Tutankhamun

48 *The Valley of the Kings with the Theban peak, el-Qurn, in the background. Image by author.*

The Saqqara Affair

It was not long into Carter's new role in Lower Egypt that his 'obstinate' personality, noted by Maspero in 1899, would be his undoing.[27] A summary of the events that unfolded in January 1905, often now called 'the Saqqara Affair', was given by Petrie in his 1931 memoir, *Seventy Years in Archaeology*. When recollecting his wife's (Hilda Petre, 1871–1956) own excavations at Saqqara in 1905, he wrote:[28]

> One Sunday some drunken Frenchmen tried to force their way into her [Petrie's] huts, and were stoutly resisted by the cook boy. They went onto the official house and began to smash furniture and fight the native guards. Carter, then inspector, was fetched, and he very rightly allowed the guards to defend themselves till the police could come.

> The indignity of letting a native resist a Frenchman weighed more than the indignity of being drunk and disorderly, in the eyes of the French Consul, who demanded an apology from Carter. With proper self-respect, Carter refused to apologise for doing his obvious duty. For this he was, on demand of the French, dismissed from the Service. This was perhaps the dirtiest act of subservience to French arrogance.'

Petrie's rather one-sided account paints Carter very favourably but some points are in need of clarification.[29] On Sunday 8th January 1905, Carter was at Saqqara with Arthur Weigall (1880–1934), and Misses Kingsford and Hansard (part of Hilda Petrie's team) when he was called to a disturbance at the Service des Antiquités' resthouse. In Carter's later account to Lord Cromer, he reported that 15 French visitors had arrived at Saqqara in a drunken state having picnicked at Memphis earlier in the day. Some then visited Petrie's excavations and caused a disturbance by trying to get into her dig house. After this they travelled across to Mariette Pasha's House (the Service des Antiquités' resthouse on the Saqqara plateau) and arranged to visit the monuments by purchasing some tickets. The ticket inspector, Es-Sayid Effendi Mohamed, sold tickets to some of them and took the party over to the Serapeum with a *gaffir*. Naturally, the *gaffir* only admitted those that had purchased tickets but those without tickets rushed the iron gate and broke it off the hinges knocking the *gaffir* to the ground. Once inside the catacombs, they were left in darkness as they had not brought any candles. The *gaffir* informed them that the Antiquities Service did not provide candles and so they demanded a refund. A fight broke out and they attacked the *gaffir* and inspector. *Reis* (foreman) Khalifa came to assist after hearing the fight break out before retreating to the resthouse to fetch Carter who was close by with Weigall. When Carter arrived, the French group had barricaded themselves into the resthouse and refused to leave when requested causing the fight to continue with rocks being thrown, one of which struck a *gaffir*.

49 *Saqqara, site of the 3rd Dynasty Step Pyramid of king Djoser and the later Serapeum catacombs of the sacred Apis Bull of Memphis. Image by author.*

This provoked Carter to give the order for his Egyptian colleagues to defend themselves using their sticks (*nabout*, a traditional marker of office in Egypt). With injuries now on both sides, the party eventually left. On leaving, Carter gave them his name and title and immediately informed the local police of the incident. The French party, of course, did the same.

The incident reached the press with even the French press noting that the party had picnicked at Memphis before arriving at Saqqara. They reported that this picnic included 12 bottles of red wine with others reporting that the party included two women and two children, though it's unclear if this implies that they were not able to fight. Of course, each party pointed the finger at the other.

Carter, naturally, reported the incident to his superior, Maspero, who was travelling in Nubia at the time. Maspero followed along closely in the national press as well as by letter with Carter himself and Émile Brugsch, (1842–1930, Maspero's deputy in the Service). A council was set up to investigate the matter and both Lord Cromer and Jules J J de la Bouliniere (the French Consul) were involved as well as representatives of the Courts. As part of this, Major Elgood carried out interviews of the Egyptian *gaffirs* at Saqqara as well as the guides with the French party. Though their official findings have never been released publicly, Carter seemed to believe that they found in his favour and wrote eagerly to colleagues telling them that he was surely to be found in the right.

However, Carter had made one big mistake, in the opinion of the Council. He had ordered his Egyptian *gaffirs* to use their *nabouts* to defend themselves. Maspero, and others, noted the problems here as he had encouraged an attack on visiting French tourists. During this period of colonial sensitivity, this was unheard of but Carter defended his decision to Maspero writing on 31st January 1905:[30]

> You mention in your letter that you do not like the idea of giving the order to defend – Nobody was more disgusted on the matter than myself – But what was one to do in such a disorderly mob, threatened and one's men knocked about?

Carter refused to accept the blame for what he felt was an unavoidable action.

Maspero, a master of diplomacy and mediator between the British and French at this time, coordinated a meeting between himself, Lord Cromer, Monsieur de la Bouliniere, and Carter to clear the air on 4th February 1905. He gave clear instructions to Carter:[31]

> It is agreed with him, and I may say with Lord Cromer, that you are to come with me tomorrow between nine and ten and pay a call on M. de la Bouliniére there to express our regrets that the order you gave brought so strong consequences. That will stop the matter which was becoming irritating, and for the rest we will arrange it together.

Maspero's tone in this letter seems regretful and one of consolation for Carter during the situation. Maspero clearly aimed to smooth things over and ensure that friendly relations would continue between the two European controlling factions in Egypt. The broader political environment is important; it was not even a year since Britain and France had signed the Entente Cordial and relations remained on a knife-edge, particularly in strategic areas of their empires. Maspero's note to Carter, significantly, did not ask Carter to apologise, instead it simply asked him to offer a, sort of, non-apology, a diplomatic tactic to appease all parties.

It is unclear if the meeting Maspero planned ever came to be. As Petrie reported later, 'Carter refused to apologise' forcing Maspero to take action. He had no choice but to relocate Carter to Tanta (94 km north of Cairo). When giving the news, Maspero added, as he had been instructed, that this was a form of punishment:[32]

> However I am authorized to tell you that this action is the consequence not of your actual action at Saqqara, but of your attitude after the event. [...] The question of excuses is settled [between de la Bouliniére and Cromer], but as you refused to do what was asked from you, you are reprimanded somewhat for it.

That same month, Carter requested three and a half months' leave to recover from the strain and stress of the events which were no doubt exacerbated by a meeting with Lord Cromer on 23rd February where he was probably further reprimanded. Maspero granted Carter's request for leave and Carter left for England shortly after. He ultimately only spent seven weeks away before returning and setting up a new base at Tanta in May 1905. In August 1905, a cache of temple equipment was uncovered by local *sebakh* diggers in Tukh el-Qaramus. The 'Tukh Treasure', as it became known, included gold and silver jewellery and vessels dated to the Ptolemaic Period. Carter went straight to the site and acquired the treasures for the Service des Antiquités before they were sold on the market. Carter seemed to have settled back into the job at hand.

However, after just a few months in Tanta, the strain finally got too much. He resented being in Tanta, and the way that he felt he had been treated and resigned from his position as Chief Inspector on 31st October 1905. In his own words to Maspero:[33]

> Owing to the late treatment I have received and the difficulties I now find while endeavouring to carry out my duties as Inspector in Chief for Lower Egypt in the Service des Antiquités I beg herewith to submit my resignation.

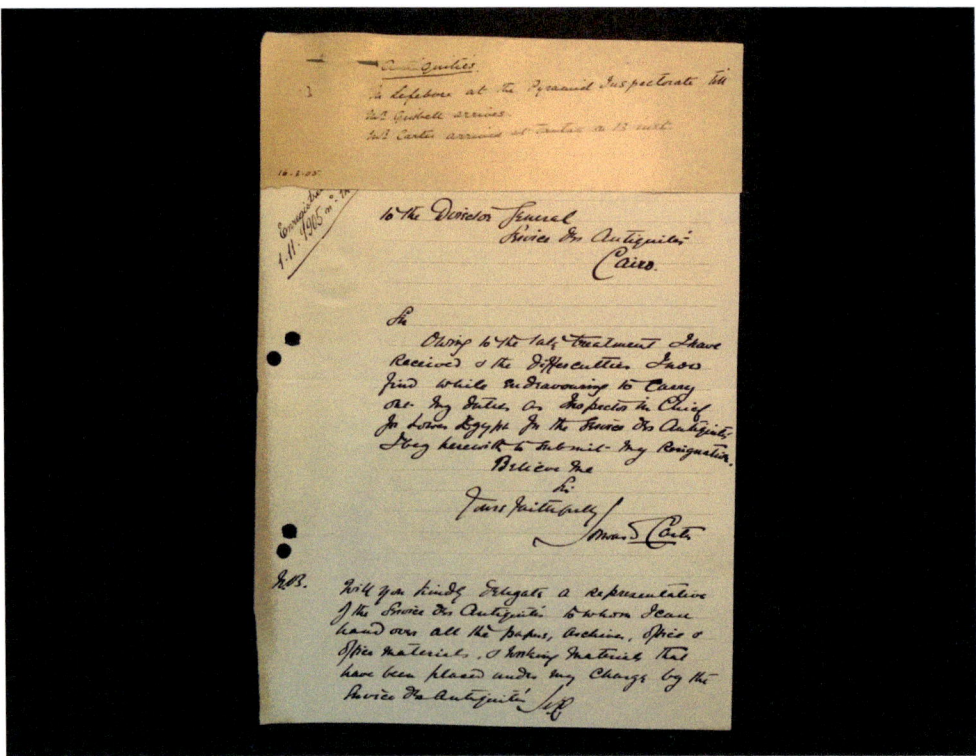

50 Carter's letter of resignation to Gaston Maspero (filed on 1st November 1905). Copyright Tony Marks.

An independent agent, 1905–1909

Carter's career at this time became less certain. He continued to reside in Egypt and relocated back to Luxor where he felt more at home. In an extraordinary act of charity, Maspero allowed Carter to move back into the Service des Antiquités rest house at Medinet Habu ('Castle Carter'), but Carter had to make his own living. At this time, gaining stable and regular archaeological work was difficult as Davis was now employing Ayrton and Jones to work on his behalf in the Valley of the Kings.

Thankfully, work came from old friends and colleagues who took pity on Carter. On 5th February 1905, Quibell, Carter's former colleague and now Chief Inspector for Upper Egypt, and his team discovered the tomb of Yuya and Thuya (KV46) with the financial support of Davis. Quibell would shortly be replaced by Weigall, but Carter was asked by Davis to paint the objects recovered from the tomb for publication. At this point, this was the most intact burial to be found in the Valley of the Kings, belonging to the great-grandparents of Tutankhamun. The tomb included rich burial goods such as boxes bearing the cartouches of the couple's son-in-law, Amenhotep III, and elaborate thrones with gold gilding. In the scientific publication of the tomb and its contents, Davis wrote of his desire that the entire contents of the tomb be retained together for display in Cairo:[34]

> Though, under the letter of my permission to explore in the "Valley of the Kings," I was not entitled to any portion of the "find," Monsieur Maspero, with a generosity common to him, offered me a share. I confess that it was a most attractive offer, but, on consideration, I could not bring myself to break up the collection which I felt ought to be exhibited intact in the Cairo Museum, where it could be seen and studied by probably the greatest number of appreciative visitors.

Until this period, a share of the excavated materials could be shared with the excavators by gift of the Service des Antiquités

51 *Chairs found in the tomb of Yuya and Thuya, painted by Howard Carter for their publication. Courtesy of Rupert Wace, UK private collection.*

in a system known as *partage*. Davis would set a precedent that would be followed for any intact (or almost intact) burial in the Valley of the Kings found afterwards.

As well as painting for archaeological projects, Carter also painted commercially. Deir el-Bahari remained a popular subject and his paintings can be found in collections around the world today.

To make a living as an independent agent, Carter often worked multiple jobs. Even after finding more stable employment (see below), the work of an archaeologist was seasonal and summers gave opportunities to engage in other paid tasks. One undertaking he, unfortunately, never completed was the copying of the festival scenes at the Luxor temple started in 1916. These scenes, showing the Opet festival, were commissioned by Amenhotep III and completed by Tutankhamun but later usurped by Horemheb during the late 18th Dynasty. The drawing of the scenes was suggested by the famous Egyptologist and philologist, Sir Alan Henderson Gardiner (1879–1963). He was so pleased to have Carter's assistance in the publication of the scenes that he described him as 'the very best artist' in 1917, telling him, 'I should like the book to be an artistic one.'[35] Gardiner later wrote, 'I want this once to do your admirable drawings real justice and to show the Americans

52   *Hoopoe in temple wall. Courtesy of Rupert Wace, UK private collection.*

that they have not the monopoly of making *éditions de luxe*.... I want our publication to be just perfect.'.[36] Ricardo Caminos (Egyptologist and epigrapher, 1915–1992) described Carter as 'an epigraphist of outstanding ability' and his work as 'epigraphy at its best' in 1976.[37] Although never published, Carter's drawings are now preserved in the Griffith Institute, University of Oxford where Gardiner's and Carter's personal papers are cared for.

Around this same time George Edward Stanhope Molyneux Herbert, the 5th Earl of Carnarvon (1866–1923, referred to as Lord Carnarvon), also took a personal interest in Egyptian archaeology. After a motoring accident in 1901, he visited Egypt regularly and, from 1906, persuaded Maspero to allow him a concession to excavate on the west bank of Luxor. Weigall, now Chief Inspector for Upper Egypt, identified some mounds at Sheikh Abdel Qurna where he felt that an amateur, as the Earl was, could not do any damage. The next season, Lord Carnarvon himself requested permission to work at Dra Abu al Naga but, before long, was out of his depth. In 1908, the Earl wrote to Weigall suggesting that 'a learned man' could work with him. Maspero, in another act of kindness, suggested Howard Carter.

Tutankhamun, 1909–1939

Carter first began working with Lord Carnarvon in 1907, but the work was seasonal, and the sites they were working on did not result in many new discoveries. Carter, therefore, maintained his connections elsewhere, including his artwork and advising museums and collectors on where to find the best pieces. It was at this time that the collection of the Amhersts that once inspired Carter as a young man in Norfolk was sold. By 1915, the family's fortunes had dried up due to mismanagement, and Lady William was forced to begin selling off the family collections. Naturally, it was Carter who was asked to catalogue the collection and to liaise with auction houses, usually Sotheby's, to make the most money for them and, where possible, go to public institutions.

53 *Just one of several drawings by Carter of the Opet Festival scenes at the Luxor Temple. Gardiner MSS. 11.5. Courtesy of the Griffith Institute, University of Oxford.*

Many of the Amhersts' Egyptian artefacts were subsequently purchased by the Metropolitan Museum of Art in New York.

By this stage in his career, Carter had built up skills as an archaeologist and artist as well as a good knowledge of the major characters working in the field at the time. He had also, unwittingly perhaps, formed a career largely around the historical characters of ancient Egypt's 18th Dynasty. Through his work in the Valley of the Kings, he had a good understanding of royal burial practices and his work as an artist had shown him that Tutankhamun, a little-known ruler in the immediate aftermath of the Amarna Period, remained curiously elusive. Before Carter could begin his search for the boy king's missing tomb, he and Carnarvon had to continue their work in other areas while Davis continued his concession in the Valley of the Kings. Between 1907 and 1914, the two men investigated Sheikh Abd el-Qurna (1907–9), Dra Abu el-Naga (1909–11), Sakha (1912), Tell el-Balamun (1913), and Hawara (1914). In 1914, Davis handed over the concession in the Valley of the Kings believing it to be exhausted and that no further tombs would be found there. The concession was quickly snatched up by Carter and Carnarvon and, other than a brief season at Meir in 1918–19, they would continue to work there for the remainder of their partnership. In 1910 Carter and Lord Carnarvon would build a grand home on Elwat el-Diban (Hill of the Flies) at the mouth of the Valley of the Kings. Carter would continue to live in this second 'Castle Carter' until shortly before his death in 1939.[38]

Carter began a systematic clearance of the main wadi bed in the Valley of the Kings clearing the limestone chips that littered the surface down to bedrock. In doing this he was able to record the presence of workers' houses in the Valley and confirm that no tombs were in those areas. He was building on the previous work of Ayrton and Jones which they had carried out under the financial support of Davis since 1905. During that time (1907), an embalming cache had been discovered, KV54, and published as the tomb of Tutankhamun. Carter recognised that the findings in KV54 did not represent a royal burial but that they did indicate that the boy king must be buried close by. By the time Carter began working under Lord Carnarvon, 61 tombs had been identified in the Valley of the Kings – the hunt was on for Tutankhamun's final resting place.

The journey of discovery took seven years until, finally, on 4th November 1922, the first step to an undiscovered tomb was found. On clearing the short stairwell down to a sealed entrance, Carter's team found a small, hastily finished, tomb filled with ancient funerary goods designed to provide for the divine king in his afterlife. It was clear, from the mummified body of the king that he died at the young age of just 18 or 19. During his short reign of about 10 years, the young ruler had restored Egypt's pantheon of deities that had been abolished by his father, Akhenaten, during what is now known as the Amarna Period. He promoted the cult of Amun again and even changed his name from Tutankhaten (Living Image of the Aten) to Tutankhamun (Living Image of Amun).

However, the famous discovery of his tomb almost never happened. The story goes that Lord Carnarvon had informed Carter that, owing to a lack of finds and funds, this would be his last season in the Valley. Carter even offered to fund this final season himself, convinced that he was close. It is suspicious, perhaps, that the steps to the tomb were found just a few days into the season. It is possible, of course, that Carter had suspected this area all along, owing to previous records by people like Ayrton and Jones – both by then deceased. Though Carter's own intuition and knowledge of the Valley's archaeology and geology should not be underestimated either.

When the sealed doorway at the foot of the stairs was revealed, Carter summoned Lord Carnarvon to join him. He cut a small hole in the sealed wall and peered through, using a candle to light his way. After moments, Carnarvon asked if he could see anything. Carter replied, 'Yes, it is wonderful'. This would later be repurposed for the press into the famous words 'Wonderful things' – but the sentiment remains the same.

Despite its small scale, the sheer number of artefacts held in the tomb meant that it would take more than ten years for Carter and his team to excavate, record, and clear it. The team led by Carter and funded by Lord Carnarvon and, after his death his wife Almina Herbert (1876–1969), included Harry Burton (1879-1940) as photographer, Arthur Mace (1874– 1928) and Alfred Lucas (1867–1945) as conservators, Newberry for the botanical remains, and Arthur Callendar (1875–1936) for engineering and logistical operations. Gardiner also took on the translation of texts from the tomb, though many remain outstanding even today. Carter was also assisted by an Egyptian team made up of many unnamed workers. Those that were named and publicly acknowledged, as usual, were those in higher positions such as the *ruasa* (sing. *reis*) Ahmed Gerigar, Gad Hassan, Hussein Abu Awad, and Hussain Ahmed Said. Little is known about their personal lives, achievements, or roles, but they were instrumental in the successful recording and careful preservation of the vast majority of what was uncovered.

The clearance of the tomb did not go ahead without problems. In 1922, Egypt gained semi-independence from British colonial rule and, naturally, took greater charge of its affairs. The Service des Antiquités remained under French administration, but nonetheless were sympathetic to Egyptian political aspirations and so decided that no objects from the tomb would leave Egypt. Though accepted by Carter and Lord Carnarvon, it is clear now that some artefacts were removed from the tomb without the knowledge of the Service, and subsequently returned on Carter's death. Lord Carnarvon had upset the authorities further by coming to an agreement on 9th January 1923 with The Times newspaper in England for exclusive rights to news of the discovery. This angered both international and national Egyptian press which were now forced to hear the latest news via the British media. This led to increasingly hostile relations between Carter and the Service, both of whom bore the brunt of the issue. This came to a head in February 1924 when Carter refused to work and closed up the tomb to experts and visitors. Following a hiatus, work resumed in early 1925, but not without some causalities in artefacts left uncared for.

Carnarvon, though causing the issue initially, died of sepsis from an infected mosquito bite in April 1923 before the tomb had even been fully explored. He never looked upon the face of Tutankhamun, or even the golden mask. His widow, Almina, of Rothschild fame and fortune, footed the bill and his death was, ironically, announced in The Times newspaper.

Carter would spend the rest of his life cataloguing and recording the finds from the tomb and would never find the time to publish the discovery scientifically, satisfying himself with some popular books for general readership. Many of the artefacts remain unpublished and understudied, even today.

As international interest in the discovery diminished, Carter faded from the public eye and become more reclusive. He died in Kensington, close to the Royal Albert Hall and Rich Terrace where he was born, on 2nd March 1939 aged 64 from cancer. He

54   *The golden mask of Tutankhamun, a representation of the divine Pharaoh in death. Made of solid gold and inlaid with precious stones, it is perhaps one of the most enduring images of ancient Egypt. Copyright Tarek Heikal, licenced under Creative Commons, CC BY-SA, via Wikimedia.*

was buried in a quiet ceremony at Putney Vale Cemetery on 6th March with a solemn crowd including Lady Evelyn Beauchamp, the daughter of Lord Carnarvon, his brother William, nephew Samuel, and a few Egyptologists. On his headstone are written the words:

> May your spirit live, may you spend millions of years, you who love Thebes, sitting with your face to the north wind, your eyes beholding happiness

These words are taken, in translation, directly from one of the alabaster vessels in the tomb of Tutankhamun, uniting the two men in their destinies and afterlives.

Today, Carter is remembered as the archaeologist who led the discovery of the tomb of Tutankhamun. But his legacy and contributions to the field of Egyptology go far beyond this, notably in archaeological recording and epigraphy. His early work as an artist and 'tracer' and later recording of the royal tombs in the Valley of the Kings are testament to this and set the standard for archaeological work at the time and for decades after. Carter's legacy is, perhaps, shown most singularly by this watercolour – EES.ART.224 – which has its own story to tell in the history of British Egyptology.

Further reading

There are many volumes written about Howard Carter and the tomb of Tutankhamun. The following have been regularly consulted in the preparation of this text and readers will find further referenced material in the endnotes.

The Griffith Institute, University of Oxford: http://www.griffith.ox.ac.uk/ [last accessed 21st March 2024].

James, T. G. H. 1992. *Howard Carter: The Path to Tutankhamun*. London: Kegan Paul International.

James, T. G. H. 1997. 'The Very Best Artist', in E. Goring, N. Reeves, and J. Ruffle (eds), *Chief of Seers: Egyptian Studies in Memory of Cyril Aldred*, London: Kegan Paul, 164–173.

Reeves, N. and, Taylor, J. 1992. *Howard Carter before Tutankhamun*. London: British Museum Press.

Riggs, C. 2022. *Treasured: How Tutankhamun Shaped a Century*. London: Atlantic Books.

For further information and resources on this book, or to find out more about the work of the EES and how you can support it, please visit https://www.ees.ac.uk or scan the QR code below:

Critical discussions

Here are a few discussion points raised by the content of this Spotlight volume. Why not read over them after reading and mull over how you might answer them? Try them out with others too.

- Carter did not begin his career in Egypt as an archaeologist, but as an artist. The important role artists played in the development of Egyptology is not always appreciated but is clear from the archives preserved at the Egypt Exploration Society. Why did art play such a significant role in early Egyptology, and why is it important to recognise this when using archives today?

- It is not clear exactly how Howard Carter created such impressive paintings like EES.ART.224 but evidence of things like pin holes and brush strokes help to reconstruct his working methods to some extent. How do you think Carter completed this painting in particular and how has archaeological recording changed today?

- Howard Carter acted on behalf of the Amherst family to secure rights to excavate at the Qubbet el-Hawa, as well as to distribute artefacts into their private collection. Carter also collected on behalf of public museums. This changed in 1922 following the discovery of the tomb of Tutankhamun. How do you feel about the broad dispersal of Egyptian heritage to collections, both private and public, around the world? What impact has this had on public understanding of ancient Egyptian culture globally, and on the study of it in Egypt today?

- The relationship between Howard Carter and the Egyptian government wore down during the excavation of the tomb of Tutankhamun from 1922. What factors led to this and what implications did this have for Egyptology afterwards?

Endnotes

1 Carter MSS vi.2.9. Griffith Institute, University of Oxford. Quoted from James 1992: 7.
2 EEF Annual Report, 1888–89.
3 EEF Annual Report, 1889–90.
4 F L Griffith incorrectly reported that the team resided in tomb 15 (see note 3). He describes the tomb as uninscribed but it is, in fact, richly decorated, belonging to the local Nomarch Bakt III. From the image (see figure 11) and description given, it seems more likely that the team resided in tomb chapel 16.
5 EES.COR.012.d.55.
6 Carter MSS vi.2.9 (page 24). Griffith Institute, University of Oxford. Quoted from James 1997: 166.
7 EES.COR.012.d.55.
8 The name of Sheikh Eid is given on page 16 of Carter's autobiographical sketch. He describes him as 'a gentle inoffensive creature, content with his lot.'. Courtesy of Tony Marks.
9 EES.COR.012.d.57.
10 Lichtheim, M. 1976. *Ancient Egyptian Literature: The Old and Middle Kingdoms.* University of California Press: Berkeley, Los Angeles, and London. Page 21.
11 Petrie, W. M. F. 1894. *Tell el Amarna*. London: Methuen & Co. Page 3.
12 Newberry, P. 1895. *El Bersheh: Part I, the tomb of Tehuti-hetep*. London: The Egypt Exploration Fund. Pages 18–19.
13 EES.COR.012.d.20 – a copy taken from W M F Petrie's diary and presented to the Committee of the Egypt Exploration Fund.
14 EES.COR.017.d.22-1.
15 Petrie MSS 1.11 – Petrie Journal 1891-82 (page 75). Griffith Institute, University of Oxford.
16 EES.COR.06.b.17-1.
17 EES.COR.01.c.03.
18 Carter MSS vi.2.9 (page 51). Griffith Institute, University of Oxford. Quoted from James 1997: 166.
19 Carter MSS vi.2.9 (page 71). Griffith Institute, University of Oxford.

20   Other assistants included Percy Brown in 1894–96, and Charles Sillem in 1896-1900.
21   See Dodson, A. Forthcoming (2025). *Thutmose III and Hatshepsut, Pharaohs of Egypt: Their Lives and Afterlives*. Cairo: AUC Press. And personal communications, Campbell Price (2024).
22   Geneva MS. 2529 (page 207) – translation from French quoted from James 1992: 70.
23   In a letter, dated 15th April 1902, to his 'Mater', Carter describes how San-Toy took the place of his gazelles but 'his ways and manners do not surpass them and his voice far from elegant. His talents tend towards gardening. He reaps but never sows; a habit that runs in the family.' Courtesy of Tony Marks.
24   Carter MSS vi.2.10. Griffith Institute, University of Oxford. Quoted from Reeves and Taylor 1992: 73.
25   Reeves, N. and Wilkinson, R. H. 1996. *The Complete Valley of the Kings*. London: Thames & Hudson. Page 108.
26   JE 46097 in Carter, H. and Newberry, P. 1904. *The Tomb of Thoutmôsis IV*. London: Archibald Constable and Co., LtD. Pages 24-38.
27   Carter, himself, would reflect at the beginning of his own autobiographical sketches: 'I have a hot temper, and that amount of tenacity of purpose, which unfriendly observance sometimes call obstinacy, and which nowadays, due to such of my idiosyncrasies, it pleases my enemies to term me as having "un mauvais caractère." Well! That I can't help!' Courtesy of Tony Marks.
28   Petrie, W. M. F. 1931. *Seventy Years in Archaeology*. London: Sampson Low, Marston & Co,. LtD. Page 192.
29   Further information, from Carter's perspective, is given in a report he compiled and now kept at the Griffith Institute, University of Oxford. Carter MSS v.148, quoted in James 1992: 99–101.
30   Quoted from James 1992: 107.
31   Carter MSS v.121. Griffith Institute, University of Oxford. Quoted from James 1992: 108.
32   Carter MSS v.125. Griffith Institute, University of Oxford. Quoted from James 1992: 112.
33   Transcribed from a copy in the collection of Tony Marks. A further

copy of Carter's letter of resignation from the Service des Antiquités can be found in the Griffith Institute, University of Oxford: Carter MSS v.147.

34   Davis, T. M. 1907. *The tomb of Iouiya and Touiyou*. London: Archibald Constable and Co., LtD. Page xxx.

35   Carter MSS v.97. Griffith Institute, University of Oxford. Quoted from James 1992: 210; James 1997: 164.

36   Carter MSS v.101. Griffith Institute, University of Oxford. Quoted from James 1992: 211; James 1997: 164.

37   Caminos, R. 1976. *Ancient Egyptian Epigraphy and Palaeography: The Recording of Inscriptions and Scenes in Tombs and Temples.* New York: The Metropolitan Museum of Art. Page 7.

38   Though considering this as his residence until 1939, he also lived in Kensington, London where he eventually died. The home at Elwat el-Diban is now open to visitors as 'Carter House' after restoration by the American Research Center in Egypt.

Index

A
Ahmose (Queen) 52, 55
Akhenaten (Pharaoh, also Amenhotep IV) 37, 40, 69, 85
Amarna (also Tell el-Amarna, el-Amarna, Akhetaten) 36–37, 43, 44–46, 69, 84–85
Amherst family 11, 15, 23–25, 44, 65, 82–83
  Amherst, Margaret Susan (Lady Amherst, nee Mitford) 11, 23
  Cecil, Lady William 65
  Tyssen-Amherst, William (Baron William Amherst Tyssen-Amherst, 1st Baron Amherst of Hackney) 11, 44–46
Awad, Hussein Abu 86
Aye (Pharaoh) 69
Ayrton, Edward 72, 79

B
Baring, Evelyn (also Lord Cromer) 64, 74, 76–77
Beni Hasan 15, 17, 19–23, 26–29, 32–37
Blackden, Marcus Worseley 19, 22, 26, 28–30, 34–35, 38–43
Brugsch, Émile 75
Buckman, Percy 25
Burton, Harry 85

C
Callendar, Arthur 85
Caminos, Ricardo 82
Carter, Amy Joyce (sister) 51
Carter, Martha Joyce (mother, nee Sands) 10
Carter, Samuel John (father) 10–13
Carter Vernet (also Verney, brother) 11, 53
Carter, William (brother) 11, 14
Castle Carter I 62–63, 79
Castle Carter II (also Carter House) 84

D
Davis, Theodore 66–67, 72, 79–80, 84
Deir el-Bahari 72, 80
  Bab el-Hosan (Tomb/Gate of the Horse) 63–65
  Temple of Hatshepsut 47–61
  Temple of Mentuhotep Nebhepetre 65
Deir el-Bersha 36–37, 39, 43, 47
Didlington Hall, Norfolk 11, 15, 23

E
Edwards, Amelia Ann Blanford 15, 23, 37, 42–43, 46
EES.ART.224 54–61
Egypt Exploration Fund (EEF, also Society) 9, 10, 15–16, 20, 23, 28, 37, 40, 42, 44, 61, 63, 65
Eid, Sheikh 37, 43
El Sheikh Said 47

F
Fraser, George Willoughby 19, 20–21, 25–26, 28, 38–43

G
Gardiner, Alan Henderson 80–82, 85
Gerigar, Ahmed 86
Griffith, Francis Llewellyn 16, 18–19, 22, 27, 37–38, 43–44
Griffith Institute, University of Oxford 11, 82

H
Hassan, Gad 86
Hatnub (quarry) 30, 36–44
Hatshepsut (Pharaoh) 47–48, 50, 53–55, 58–59, 65, 72
Herbert, George Edward Stanhope Molyneux (also Lord Carnarvon, 5th Earl of Carnarvon) 82–88
Horemheb (Pharaoh) 69

J
Jones, Ernest Harold 72, 79

L
Lucas, Alfred 85
Luxor Temple 80–83

M
Mace, Arthur 85
Maspero, Gaston 61–62, 65, 73, 75–79, 82

N
Newberry, John 25
Newberry, Percy 15, 17, 19–28, 37–43, 47, 61, 67, 85

P
Paget, Rosalind 53, 55
Paterson, Emily 40, 43
Petrie, Hilda (nee Urlin) 73–74
Petrie, William Matthew Flinders 26, 37–38, 40, 44, 46, 73–74, 77
Poole, Reginald Stuart 18

Q
Qubbet el-Hawa 65
Quibell, James Edward 61, 72, 79

S
Said, Hussain Ahmed 86
Senseneb (Queen) 54–55
Service des Antiquités de l'Égypte 47, 61, 72, 74–75, 77–79, 86
Swaffham, Norfolk 10–11, 13

T
Tutankhamun (also Tutankhaten) 9, 37, 40, 69, 79–80, 82–88
Tuthmosis III (Pharaoh) 66, 72
Tuthmosis II (Pharaoh) 54
Tuthmosis I (Pharaoh) 54–55, 72
Tuthmosis IV (Pharaoh) 67–72

V
Valley of the Kings 9, 10, 65, 67, 72–73, 79–80, 83–84, 88

KV20 (Hatshepsut) 72
KV34 (Tuthmosis III) 66
KV35 (Amenhotep II) 65
KV38 (Tuthmosis I) 72
KV42 66
KV43 (Tuthmosis IV) 67–71
KV44 72
KV45 72
KV46 (Yuya and Thuya) 79
KV54 84
KV60 72
KV62 (Tutankhamun) 84–87

W
Weigall, Arthur 74, 79, 82